To Hilda
Thanks for your
Support!

JOURNEY TO THE
MOUNTAIN
WITHIN

Healing Today's Youth

LUIS R. RUAN

ISBN: 1489535314
ISBN 13: 9781489535313

JOURNEY TO THE MOUNTAIN WITHIN

DEDICATION

I dedicate this book to my son's, Gabriel and Nico Ruan. I love you from here to God.
And to my loving father who resides with my ancestors in the spirit world. This is for you!

FORWARD TO

Journey to the Mountain Within

LUIS R. RUAN IS one of this country's leading youth counselors, music teachers, and community healers; I don't write this to be flippant or to exaggerate. He's also a martial arts practitioner, a wilderness instructor, Native American sweat lodge participant, and Boyle Heights/East Los Angeles community organizer —the area with more street gangs and more Mexicans than any other in the United States.

And he's my friend, mentor, and brother of the heart.

Journey to the Mountain Within is about the solid, mineral-rich and complex center we all carry inside that we can tap into—that stone spirit latent in our bones that holds our truths, our stories, but also our ties to all life, the ancestors, the cosmos, past, present, and future.

My *tocayo* (meaning namesake, the old Nahuatl word that is affectionately used throughout Mexico) has written a practical step-by-step book on mentoring and youth engagement, drawing upon methods that only one who has spent years doing this work can grasp and convey— usually with hard days and nights, hard decisions, and many hard losses.

And Luis has the experience and understanding to bring this forward like few can.

This is also a book about spirit, courage, respect, about the glue that connects all humanity, all generations, all life, all our relations—about real love for one another, for family, for community—and how accessing these can help anyone get through the most troubled times and troubled places.

Born in the United States, Luis is of Purepecha indigenous descent from Michoacan, Mexico. He has been a font of native knowledge, medicine, and teachings for years. When I met him, he was a probation officer in the Orange County Juvenile Probation system. This was around 1995 and we learned that we were both into our indigenous roots and traditions (mine's into the Mexika and Raramuri—also known as Tarahumara—from Chihuahua, Mexico). We also learned that we loved to help turn the lives around of some of the most lost young people, in gangs, in lockups, or on drugs.

Over the years, Luis and I worked together in Boyle Heights, the Northeast San Fernando Valley, with ex-prisoners, and recovering addicts. We managed talks at the Pine Ridge and Navajo Reservations. With my wife Trini, we helped found two Sweat Lodges in the Northeast Valley. And Luis was one of our key supporters, instructors, and performers at Tia Chucha's Centro Cultural & Bookstore, the cultural space/workshop center that Trini and I helped create in Sylmar, California.

You'll love this Journey, this book. I recommend it highly, not just for the wisdom contained, but also for the stories, the images, and personal insights.

There's nothing more to say but, "read on."

—Luis J. Rodriguez ~January 1, 2012 ~
San Fernando, California

Luis J. Rodriguez is the author of:
Always Running: *La Vida Loca, Gang Days in L.A.*
His latest book is the sequel,
It Calls You Back: An Odyssey Through Love, Addiction, Revolutions, and Healing

INTRODUCTION

Ten years have come and gone like a swift wind...
Many things have changed since I started writing this book. The
preliminary version of *Journey to the Mountain Within* looked nothing like this. It began as a step-by-step manual on how to work with
challenged youth, and grew from there.

Based on my frustration working within the juvenile justice system and marginalized communities, it was easy to fill the pages of
my first draft. My intent was to provide information that would be
helpful to parents, teachers, social workers, probation officers, and
law enforcement, offering an alternative perspective that addressed
the basic core motivators contributing to juvenile delinquency.

I asked my friend, renowned author, Luis Rodriguez, to read the
first draft. He suggested I add stories about my experiences, not to
make it so technical, and to develop it into a narrative. I added stories and changed the entire direction of the book spending another

four years changing and developing stories about my encounters with youth. But that was not enough; I added imagery and my own personal stories.

The remnants of the original draft are almost gone. In its place is a soul-searching reflective memoir of my experiences working inside juvenile correctional facilities, coordinating challenging backpacking excursions, facilitating workshops with adult inmates, working in under-represented Latino communities and Native American Nations across the United States and Canada.

My parents were my first teachers…

A contributing element of my philosophy in this book is based on my upbringing; I grew up in a disenfranchised Mexican-American working-class community in National City, California. My parents were my first teachers. They exemplified the art of generosity and community support. People would come to our home to seek advice from them. Family members who had marital or family problems would visit my parents, knowing they would receive guidance.

I remember the constant flow of familiar faces, seeking the counsel of my mother and father about their everyday problems ranging from dealing with divorce to understanding their troubled teens. We often had teenagers staying with us because their parents needed to keep them away from the trouble they had created in their own cities. They needed to *lay low* until they were ready to return. My mother and father were given the responsibility of getting them back on track. The generosity of my parents was expressed in so many different ways. I saw almost every conceivable human problem walk into my home.

During the mid 1970's when I was thirteen, I remember my dad barbequing *carne asada* (thin grilled marinated steak) in the front yard of our home. I avoided him that day knowing he would inevitably make us busy with Saturday chores. If he noticed any of his six kids not helping out, he would create projects for us; if he saw a young person just standing around, family relation or not, he would put them to work. He created such a dominant presence that everyone seemed to accept his authority, fearful to oppose his requests; he could make dogs cry.

You see, my father was a Sergeant during World War II. Consequently, he would run Saturday morning chores like a quasi-military operation; he could not accept unproductive behavior. Being a free-spirited laid-back young man, I did what I could in my creative power to stay clear of those monotonous, and sometimes fruitless, work assignments.

That afternoon, my mother sent me to the corner store (as I was often her errand boy) to buy some tomatoes. As I was slowly walking back to the house, I saw someone walking on the opposite end of the block: a tall, lean, swarthy, homeless Vietnam Veteran with a scruffy beard, thick, uncombed, shoulder length hair and wearing a soiled green army jacket. He was walking aimlessly with his head tilted toward the ground with the look of a broken man without any life in his eyes.

I could see him slowly making his way in my direction past our neighbor's house. I opened the small chain-linked gate and walked the walkway through my front yard to the side door avoiding the crew of sisters angrily mopping and cleaning the living room. I went into the kitchen, bathed in the spices and aromas of my mother's world, and handed her the tomatoes she needed for her red *salsa*. Unacknowledged, I took the trash out. Deciding to stay invisible, I went into the front yard pretending to help my father with the barbequing.

As I looked out the door, there he was, the homeless Vietnam Vet peacefully talking to my father. I silently watched as my dad handed him a thick, well-packed burrito my mom had meticulously created. He was on the outside of our three-foot fence and my dad was inside our yard and they were eating my mother's burritos. They stood two feet away from each other, eating their steaming burritos in silence, looking like two men who understood each other. I just stood there watching the amazing scene. It was almost as if they had an unspoken language connecting them to one another, the trauma, and the experience of fighting in the wars. After the man finished eating, he humbly shook my father's hand and walked away. I never saw him in our neighborhood again, and I would never forget my father's kind gesture.

What I had witnessed was my father expressing a simple act of compassion, a side of him I rarely saw. At that moment I realized that my father, worn-out from the many years of supporting his large family, had a spiritual quality masked by his hardships. Underneath his thick, rough exterior was a man capable of great kindness. Beyond his intimidating personality was a compassionate soul. What became evident was that my father, while seemingly detached and unapproachable, had a great capacity for understanding the human condition. He became my first role model for compassionate behavior.

After the homeless Vietnam Vet walked away, my dad turned to me and asked with a stern face, "Don't you have something to do?" We both went back to our routine.

Growing up, I witnessed many more examples of this kind of community social work. My parents were a great team in helping those who had lost their way. They were self-made community social workers who devoted themselves to supporting our extended family, neighbors, and friends. They were the Elders who accepted their role in their society and promoted positive family values, impacting their family for generations, inspiring their children to become socially conscious.

As I grew older, I realized I had followed a similar path of becoming a community healer. My involvement with social service began to unfold and mirrored my parents' efforts and soon became my career. As it turned out, I was well prepared and easily transitioned into a career working with disenfranchised youth. From my parents I learned that some young people are able to live successfully while others come into this world with hardships waiting for them, and these are the youth I needed to help.

Philosophy from experience...

In this book, I share with you personal stories along with true events that occurred within my inner circles. In some cases, I was asked to share these stories in hopes that parallel experiences might help to offer insight. Many of these individuals have successfully moved on with their lives, and a few of them are in the spirit world. My intent is to give a personal perspective of youth and community issues without dishonoring the people who have crossed my path. To protect the identity of my clients, names, places, and events have been altered to prevent attracting unnecessary attention, rising from the events of their past.

My clients and their stories have taught me many valuable lessons that will be passed on in this book. These lessons come from the hundreds of individuals who have experienced forms of unresolved trauma, physical, sexual, and emotional abuse, domestic violence, and abandonment. I have learned that many of these young people were raised behind the walls of juvenile hall, correctional camps, foster homes, drug rehabs, and prisons due to improper counseling, guidance, and the lack of resources. On the other hand, there are stories of success based on resiliency, community, and family support. In this field, to witness such transformation is one of the best rewards one can receive.

Yet, the individuals who were not able to cross that threshold of success and transformation became my best teachers. Often, society had dismissed these young people as *losers* or *failures*, yet they broke my heart with stories of survival and unspeakable hardship.

Their stories told, that from the very beginning of their lives, their paths went against the grain of what is normal and attainable to have a healthy, productive life. Ultimately, I learned that to be more effective as a counselor and healer, I needed to learn how to work both inside and outside of the system. I needed to utilize cultural constructs and social paradigms to enhance my effectiveness.

Climbing the mountain of self-doubt

Writing this book has been one of the biggest challenges of my life. There were moments when I went to a place of self-doubt that froze my creativity and my passion to complete this work. These were times when I needed to follow my own advice... teaching young people to do their best and go beyond adversity cornered such doubtful thoughts.

I had spent my career encouraging youth not to quit. When hitting the wall of frustration and fatigue, I would find creative means to encourage them to reach the *Summit of their Potential*. Such memories made me want to practice what I preached. I realized that only by encouraging myself, was I able to rid my mind of those self-defeating thoughts.

Who is this book for?

This book is for the parent who is having problems with their son or daughter. It is for the educator who wants to do their best to work with their students. It is for the social worker or probation officer who is looking for alternatives in dealing with young people. It is for the college student who wants to go into the social service work world and understand the complexities of our youth. It is for the individual who wants to read a story about a man who learned how to work with youth outside the confines of the system. It is about what my clients have taught me through their struggles and experiences.

In this book, I share more than twenty-five years of experience serving a broad range of communities: Santa Ana, San Diego, East Los Angeles, South Central LA, San Fernando Valley, British Columbia, and various Native American Nations. Having a connection with the individuals throughout these communities has provided me with the insight and has made me a better counselor, teacher, parent, and human being. My intent is to bring forth an understanding of a creative approach in dealing with the struggles of disenfranchised communities and youth.

I share all this with you with an open heart.

CHAPTER I

THREE MENTORS

WHEN I THINK BACK on my childhood, I see my mother in the kitchen. Most, if not all of my memories have her busily moving about, making food for us, drinking *te de limon* (Mexican lemon grass tea) with one of her sisters, or washing dishes after a delicious meal. We lived so close to the Mexican border that I hardly had to squint my eyes to see the bright lights of Tijuana homes scattered across its hills and valleys. Rumor had it you could hear Mariachi music if you listened closely enough to the breeze. My home was my sanctuary.

My father, Luis Ramiro Ruan, Sr., was born and raised in National City, California. He had relatives in the San Diego area, East Los Angeles, Tijuana and Michoacán, Mexico. My mother, Eliacer Chavoya, was originally from a small rural village in Jalisco, Mexico. She had quite a few relatives in National City as well as all over the U.S. Southwest and in Jalisco.

There were always family and friends over at the Ruan household. We often had relatives from Central Mexico staying with us.

1

My home was a way-station for relatives who were traveling to different parts of the United States to work.

My father worked as a machinist for Rohr Aircraft, a company that played a major role in the development of civilian and military air transportation. My mother had an even more challenging job as a homemaker who, in addition to having the responsibility of six energetic children, also managed a constant flow of visiting relatives, as well as a father-in-law in constant need of her care.

At that time, the County of San Diego was a prosperous military community where the Navy had a dominant presence. From my neighborhood I could see the naval shipyard with antiquated battleships that were being repaired after years of loyal service. San Diego had many attractions with its beautiful beaches, sunny weather, the world-famous San Diego Zoo, Sea World, as well as impressive scenery. Unfortunately, the Latino community never seemed to benefit from much of the revenue generated by these attractions. Instead, were deprived of community resources and burdened by the heavy police presence looming around our neighborhoods; a constant, stinging reminder of our situation. Drugs were easy to get but effective youth programs were hard to find. The combination of poverty and police presence made me see the streets of National City as an unfriendly place to survive.

I was a shy, curious, independent, and an easy-going kid who did not possess the aggressive instinct for street fighting. I had gotten into scrapes with several neighborhood youth and, on a few occasions, was beaten up pretty badly by fearless and experienced fighters. I noticed that the kids who possessed that fighting spirit were the same ones who got into trouble and began their progression into the juvenile justice system, as they got older; I knew I did not want to be one of those kids. I knew there had to be something better in life than getting into trouble with the law; that "something better" became my involvement in Japanese Karate.

I was an adolescent captivated with the exotic mystique of martial arts. Many of my daydreams consisted of wishing I lived in Japan or China so I could learn from the great masters. I imagined developing into a Martial Arts expert like my heroes at that time: Benny "Jet" Urquidez, a kick-boxing champion, full-contact karate champion Bill "Superfoot" Wallace, and the late martial arts action star and founder of Jeet Kune Do, Bruce Lee.

I watched all of the Bruce Lee movies many times and was a loyal fan of the syndicated *Kung Fu* television series that aired weekly in the late seventies. After watching these movies and television shows, I would often go into my backyard, and when I knew no one was watching, kicked trash cans pretending to be Bruce Lee fighting against evil villains. My loyal companion and best friend, a German shepherd named Bruno, shared my enthusiasm by jumping, yelping, and barking as I kicked, punched, and defeated my imaginary opponents.

Several months of constant pestering, combined with my obvious love for Karate, finally convinced my parents to take me to a Karate school. They said that I could only attend under the following conditions: it was my responsibility to find an affordable school location, agree to be more helpful around the house, and become a better brother towards my siblings. The last condition was the hardest one for me because being nice to four demanding sisters and one younger brother was going to be awkward and difficult.

I knew I was not always the best brother, I became motivated to improve my behavior in order to do something unique and with purpose.

Beginning Karate: A call to Adventure

When I was twelve years old, I began taking Karate classes at El Toyon Recreation Center in National City. My favorite nights were on Wednesdays when I was taught a Japanese style Karate, called *Wada Kai* by John Murphy. Sensei Murphy had earned his black belt while stationed in Japan as a military police officer during the Korean War. After his honorable discharge, he settled in Chula Vista, California where he worked as a butcher. He taught at the *dojo* (school of training in Japanese martial arts) in National City and across the border in Tijuana, Mexico. He was my first mentor, outside of my family.

We were a bunch of working class kids who were mesmerized with his fancy kicks and athletic movements. He taught us the fundamentals of karate and we were eager to learn these exotic fighting skills. As a member of the Army Military Police, Sensei Murphy taught us discipline and we were excited to learn.

For a Mexican kid like me, taking part in this Karate class was a rare opportunity and it was the turning point in my life. I genuinely enjoyed the entire Karate experience: the *dojo*, the camaraderie, and the physical training. I was in a strange new world that was mysterious and magical, I felt I belonged. With Martial Arts, I was home.

JOURNEY TO THE MOUNTAIN WITHIN

◎ ◎ ◎

Finding my mentor: Terry Crook

Very soon, we had to move to a new location. Out of thirty students, only five of us continued with our training at the new *dojo*. Sensei Murphy continued training us for the next year. He had been teaching at another *dojo* in Tijuana, Mexico and became too busy for us. He turned us over to one of his students, Terry Crook, a young Vietnam Veteran who was dedicated to the art. Terry had been Sensei Murphy's assistant and became our new teacher.

Within a year, Terry was elevated to a black-belt status and became our official instructor. We were grateful because he had a positive relationship with not only us as students, but also with our parents. Terry was nearly six-feet tall and built like a college linebacker with a slight resemblance to the actor Viggo Mortensen. Besides his robust exterior, he had a contagious sense of humor, able to balance discipline and fun with his students.

After a few months as a black-belt instructor, people began hearing about the *dojo* and more students joined. His students were from multicultural ancestry: Filipino, Mexican, Samoan, Guamanian, and Caucasian. It was a family of diverse individuals who shared a common love for martial arts. Most of the *dojo's* members were older teenagers and some grown men and women.

Cuahtli Karate Club

Our *dojo* was a fixed-up garage adjacent to a house belonging to Deputy Sheriff John Douglas, a black belt in Wada Kai. It was a decent-sized area with the main garage door permanently closed shut. A regular house door was built in to serve as the main entrance. Inside, from wall-to-wall, was a thick, gray *Everlast* Martial Arts mat. Large mirrors covered the left-side wall and a heavy punching bag hung from the ceiling in the far right-side of the room. On the opposite wall was a picture of our school name and emblem: *Cuahtli Karate Club.*

Cuahtli means eagle in the ancient *Nahuatl language (Uto-Aztecan linguistic group),* the main native language in Mexico. This symbol represented an Aztec Eagle Warrior who was part of the elite warrior societies for the Aztec empire, similar to U.S. Special Forces. Sensei Murphy picked the name *Cuahtli* because he taught many students in Mexico and wanted a symbol that honored ancient Mexican culture and exemplified the Martial Arts spirit.

My brother and I were fortunate to have the opportunity to experience such diversity. Here was John Douglas, a Deputy Sheriff, who cared enough about his community to open his home to kids like us. Along with our training and physical challenges, there was music and culture in the home. He was a talented musician who loved to perform Elvis Presley songs on his keyboard and guitar. On occasion, he would invite all of us into his living room where he would sing a repertoire of Elvis Presley's greatest hits.

Captivated by his musical abilities, he entertained us and we were reminded that there were other ways to escape the harshness of the world.

The Dojo Experience

I remember the *dojo* being a place where many of us could practice to perfect our skills in karate. It was an exciting environment made up of young and dedicated martial artists. Every Tuesday and Thursday night, after all our training, we would spar against one another. The sparring was interesting because the young men and women had a lot of heart. You could see by the way they fought, that many of them were experienced street fighters at one time in their lives. The ability to improve as a fighter was heightened because of this reality. In retrospect, the sparring resembled a mixed martial arts match, but without the ground fighting derived from Brazilian Jujitsu and wrestling.

During that time of martial arts evolution in the U.S., ground fighting was not as popular as it is today. The *dojo* fighting experience was a time to test what we learned and to develop our techniques, timing, and speed. Looking back on those years, I had my share of bloody lips, cuts to the face, and bruises on almost every part of my body. We always bowed to each other before any bout as a gesture of respect and we did the same afterward. I don't recall anyone losing their temper at the Cuahtli *Dojo*. Terry was helpful at maintaining a positive attitude of learning during the sparring sessions.

During the mid-seventies, many martial art schools in the San Diego area were primarily focused on tournament point karate, a competition based on gaining points from striking specific areas of the body, where kicks and punches are faster, but controlled to avoid injuries. Terry geared our sparring sessions to be closer to an actual street confrontation. He wanted us to become accustomed to knowing how it felt to get hit. Through this approach we developed essential fighting skills to utilize in life threatening situations. Terry stressed that these skills were never to be abused. Instead, he taught us that Karate was about developing character, the building of a strong mind and body, not for street violence.

The group consisted of martial artists who were disciplined and talented individuals like Lap Napoleon: a trim, six-foot Samoan who had incredible skill as a fighter, as well as a creative sense of humor. Where some people have a six-pack on their stomach; Lap had a seven-pack on his! There was an odd baseball sized protrusion between his abs and his upper chest; he once let me punch it when he caught me staring at it – it was like punching a brick wall.

Reny and Resty Endozo were also great fighters. Resty was the younger of the two and wasn't as talkative as his older brother, but approachable – we spent a lot of time sparring together. He had a stinging side kick that once took the air out of my stomach. Reny, on the other hand, was known for his flexibility and was like a rubber band with his kicks and often complimented Lap's humor.

Then there was Alfredo Perez, a young man who lived in my neighborhood, loved martial arts, and was very enthusiastic. I once rode my bike near his house and witnessed his mom chasing him with a straw broom attempting to take a whack at him.

She was yelling things in Spanish while trying to get an accurate swing. Alfredo was jumping and dodging her like a skilled alley cat laughing and saying, "No mama...no mama!" He eventually stopped out of respect and let his mother hit him on the shoulder. He smiled at me and pretended to be in pain. Alfredo was a sturdy capable street fighter but still had a respectful demeanor towards his mother. His younger brother Richie also trained with us.

There were many others. James Saludares, a robust Filipino who also played football at my high school, Sweetwater High, built like a defensive lineman. Tony Pablo was a quiet, hard working, engaging fighter who always showed respect towards everyone. We also had Rick Turner, a young actor, who was slightly blind, but a talented fighter with well-defined abdominal muscles that reminded me of a turtle shell.

And I can't forget Tisha, Mr. Murphy's teenage daughter. Tisha was of above average height with long straight golden brown hair and an appealing physical appearance. She was a polished and fearless fighter who frequently beat me up during my early days. Even though she was a girl, she earned everyone's respect because of her skills and courage. When I was younger, she was very present in the *dojo*. She then took a break from training and returned when I was older and taller. Terry and Sensei Murphy instructed me to spar with her and I wanted to give her a good challenge. I remembered all those times she was difficult to fight, and struck terror in her opponents.

During the sparring session that followed, I was faster and stronger than in my younger days. She was getting frustrated with me and I became overconfident. After a favorable exchange of kicks and punches, I walked away with an arrogant grin thinking the match was over, giving her my back.

Well, the match was not over. I turned and looked at Reny, Resty, Alfredo, and my brother all sitting crossed-legged. They all wore big smiles and I thought they were smiling at me, so I gave them a confident sparkling grin. Suddenly, I felt Tisha swiftly grab the back neck collar of my karate uniform. Her other hand grabbed the lower back area of my belt, and with her right back leg she delivered a front leg sweep and had me dangling in the air before she dropped me like a pancake. My karate buddies could not stop laughing. Terry and Sensei Murphy turned away and grinned. I learned a valuable lesson that evening.

Tisha and her brother Shawn dedicated most of their training at our sister school in Tijuana, where there were other great martial artists in training. I remember this guy named Nacho with curly dark brown hair, able to jump high and execute extremely complex aerial kicks. He was a person of very few words but able to provoke terror in his opponents. Another martial artist was Diego, a swift and effective black belt fighter who everyone looked up to, well known for his leg sweeps that often left his opponents stunned.

◎ ◎ ◎

Connecting with my Mentor

My brother Carlos and I were consistently the youngest students and never felt athletic enough or as outgoing as the older guys. We were shy and humbled by an unassuming Mexican upbringing. However, Terry made us feel like we were an integral part of the school. He spent equal amounts of time with us as with the older and more dynamic fighters. He gave us special attention, volunteering to drive us to the *dojo*.

This was timely because my parents were going through transportation challenges and my mother was the only driver in the family. For most of my youthful years my parents owned an old root beer brown Ford station wagon that often needed repairs. He knew it was not easy for my parents to raise a large family and to drive my brother and me across town twice a week. Terry eventually offered to pick us up every Tuesday and Thursday and take us to class and my parents were relieved to have that support from him. For my Mexican parents, a person who had appropriate manners and knew how to communicate socially was held in high regard; for this my parents liked Terry and he earned their trust.

For the next four years, Terry was our transportation, taking us across town to the *dojo*. He would drive from northeast San Diego to my neighborhood in southern San Diego County across to the northeast section of National City. On weekends, he would take us to Karate tournaments. After awhile, other kids in my neighborhood wanted to join, but they did not have the money or transportation. Terry patiently drove as many of us who could fit into his golden-brown, detailed Volkswagen Baja Bug. Whenever we heard the distinct humming sound of his Volkswagen down the street, my brother and I, and other kids from the neighborhood would run to meet at my house and then frantically squeeze our way into his tiny car.

At times there might have been four or five of us piled into his Volkswagen, in the 70's seatbelt laws were not as stringent. From the drive to the *dojo* and back to the house, Terry entertained us with his good-natured humor and there was never a dull moment. He would share funny stories and tell jokes. All the silliness and joking around during the drive changed once we got to the *dojo* where focus and discipline replaced humor and fun. We knew our training was to be taken seriously.

Terry welcomed all young men from the neighborhood to the karate classes. People in my neighborhood associated him and his Baja Bug with us and karate. Anytime he drove on my street on Coolidge Avenue, people just knew and understood what he was doing in our community. My neighborhood was the type where everyone knew everyone. Gossip was its own language in National City, except it was more often done over *pan dulce* (Mexican sweet bread) and in whispers than aloud on the street. No one gossiped or wondered about Terry; his efforts with us neighborhood kids earned him a silent acceptance and appreciation. This relationship lasted for five years.

◎ ◎ ◎

Dojo Changes

Nothing lasts forever, and unfortunately for us, John Douglas decided to move and rent out his home. The agreement was that we would continue to maintain the *dojo* but the new tenants did not respect our space. Our training equipment was misplaced and used without our permission. The renters started putting their personal belongings on our mats. The final straw was when they let their dog leave fresh excrement in the middle of our mat. We knew it was time to stop using the *dojo*. Terry decided to move out and take us to another location, a karate school called Tracy Kenpo Karate in the city of El Cajon. Some of his students continued to train with Terry at the new location, but for most of us it was too far of a drive.

By this time, I was seventeen and in high school. Every now and then, I would train with Terry at his new studio. I remember one time he invited me to spar with some of the advanced students at Tracy Karate. I fought against a black belt that was much older than me. As we got into what I thought was a fair sparring match, my opponent became upset. Before I knew it, he took off his gloves and insisted I fight him bare-handed. The head instructor Dick Willet intervened and told his student to calm down. The instructor separated us and asked us to kneel and meditate away from each other. In that time, my opponent appeared to calm down.

Terry approached and helped adjust my belt "Go ahead, and kick his ass!" he said. "He has a big mouth, and you can take him." My opponent had a reputation of having a bad attitude and a short-temper. I wasn't surprised to hear this direction from Terry. I returned to the center of the mat to continue sparring. Immediately, my opponent started getting more and more angry. I listened to my teacher and fought my opponent without anger in my heart.

Looking back, I realized this experience was a training session for me. I learned that in order to be effective when dealing with people under the influence of rage, one must remain focused on their technique without being distracted by the opponent's anger. At that moment, I realized I was no longer a shy twelve year old adolescent who was picked on by neighborhood bullies. I had transformed into an agile, capable and experienced fighter.

Terry was always able to keep us grounded. During another occasion, my brother Carlos and I went to his studio for a sparring session. Terry asked me to spar with him. At that time I was 5'8", weighing about 145 pounds. Terry was three inches taller and easily carried about twenty-five pounds more muscle than me and clearly more experienced in karate. However, at that moment none of that mattered since I was so eager to prove to my teacher I had evolved as a martial artist. As I was putting on my gloves and foot gear, I remembered, how in my younger years, I was terrified to fight Terry. He had these fast, hard kicks that easily caused damage to the receiver.

When we began the sparring match, Terry had a look of amusement on his face. He let me execute several fancy face-level kicks which he easily dodged and blocked. In the next interaction we exchanged more kicks and punches. I remember the patient look in his eye as if he were up to something. I didn't care; I wanted to show him that I was not a kid anymore, and I was capable of becoming a worthy opponent during the sparring match.

Before making contact I decided I would come in with a left fake front-kick and then a swift right-leg roundhouse-kick to his head. I wanted to keep him guessing as to what my next move would be. Terry quickly read and predicted my moves and placed a forceful, stepping side-kick to my stomach, sending me flying through the air. All I could remember was how I felt as I flew across the room, landing flat on my back as if I had been kicked off a horse.

Terry walked towards me with a warm fatherly smile and extended his hand helping lift me back up on my feet. I smiled; he laughed with amusement and said, "Trying to beat the old man, huh?" He walked away with a low chuckle. After the sparring, everyone was in high spirits.

As I looked around the *dojo*, I was reminded of how Terry had invested years of training and hours of his own personal time in me. When I think of what a good mentor is, I see him driving the neighborhood kids to karate practice, asking nothing in return. People like him, who work so hard to connect with youth, truly leave lasting impressions. Such good people were hard to find then, but are even harder to find for today's youth.

Third Mentor
Orned "Chicken" Gabriel

The third mentor who crossed my path was Kenpo Karate instructor, Orned Gabriel, the head instructor at United Karate Federation. He was of medium height and an athletically built African-American. Everyone fondly called him by his nickname, *Chicken*. At first I thought it was because of the way he fought, fast hands and fast kicks. But the story was told that when he was a baby, his father said he sounded like a chicken when he cried, and the name stuck. In the seventies, his studio was located on Highland Avenue in National City. Most of the martial artist students at my high school, Sweetwater High, trained in Wadai Kai, or Kenpo. Martial Artists from both studios had a lot of respect for one another.

During the early eighties Chicken moved his studio to Spring Valley, located east of National City. At the time, I was an unemployed full-time student training in the backyard of my parent's house and couldn't afford to pay the monthly fees. Hearing of my situation, he told me not to worry and generously invited me to train for free. I was fortunate to receive his mentorship and generosity.

Chicken combined meditation and Eastern philosophy with demanding physical workouts. Music was incorporated into his trainings, teaching rhythm along with footwork. He created an environment that was positive and inviting. He also had a unique way of making everyone feel welcomed as soon as you stepped into his studio. In a deep engaging voice, he would greet me as if he had not seen me for a long time, "Hey, Luees! Where you been, man? Good to see you, brother... Ready to work hard and train?"

His charismatic personality drew a lot of people to him. Those of us who trained at the studio saw him as a solid role model and we were like an extended family. Lots of love was felt through his positive interaction with students. *Chicken* was not only a martial art instructor; he was a life coach as well. He just made you feel good, helped build you up and made you feel like you could do anything; he made us believe in ourselves. Not only were our bodies in training but our attitudes and minds as well. In his lifetime he has taught martial arts to almost 10,000 students, a great teacher. His most well-known student was the former ten-time World Point Karate Champion, Steve "Nasty" Anderson.

...young people need a place where they belong

The reason I mention these stories is because as an adolescent, karate allowed me to escape from the negative elements of violence, drugs, and alcohol. From twelve until twenty-two years of age, I had three main mentors in martial arts: Sensei John Murphy, Terry Crook, and Orned "Chicken" Gabriel. While others my age were getting into trouble with the law, I was mostly going to Cuahtli Karate Dojo, Tracy's Kenpo, United Karate Federation, or training in my backyard. Karate positively occupied my time and took me to another world outside of my neighborhood. In these places, I was respected and was part of something that was healthy and supportive. These mentors gave me encouragement and made me feel that I was capable of greatness. This was communicated through their actions and words.

These experiences with all my mentors taught me about the importance of positive role models. As we go through life, mentors will come into our lives to help guide us and to assist us in reaching our potential. The mentor might come to us in different forms; it could be someone familiar to us or someone from a different ethnic background. A mentor could be any gender or age. What matters is that when the mentor appears in someone's life, the individual is ready to accept and learn from them. Terry was a mentor who left a deep impression on many young men and women at Cuahtli Karate Club. As I got older, more mentors crossed my path and assisted in shaping my destiny.

Traits of a Positive Mentor

1. Wise: has overcome personal challenges and is committed to living a healthy lifestyle
2. Reliable: follows through with their word
3. Commitment: willing to commit at least a year of mentoring to be effective and develop trust
4. Relentless: has faith in the person they are helping
5. Authentic: an example of walking a positive and healthy lifestyle
6. Consistent: always available
7. Respectful: clear personal boundaries
8. Tolerant: accepting diversity

Call to Action: Become a Mentor

Many of our young people are growing up without the support of one or both parents and all too often look to the streets for a sense of community. There are negative forces out there that are stealing away our children from their own potential. I have come across hundreds of youth who, with the right guidance and support, could have excelled in any chosen profession. I often hear people say that we need more jails and stricter law enforcement to deal with today's youth issues. Instead, part of the solution is to have an abundance of positive and consistent mentors available who can guide our youth onto healthier paths. Young people who have been positively impacted by mentors will undoubtedly do the same for others with even more passion and understanding.

It's easy to become a mentor. One could start mentoring youth in their own neighborhood, in a different neighborhood, in after-school programs or by joining an organized mentorship program. Our youth are starving for the guidance of positive mentors. In order to excel, all young people need direction from a positive influence. Mentoring isn't expensive; it takes time and commitment and is one of the most powerful, commendable deeds an individual can accomplish.

I see people daily who have so much to give, who are smart, talented and could be a positive influence on a teen. From my own experience, I know the young people I worked with observed everything I did and mimicked my behavior.

I have learned that it is important for all people to have a purpose. In youth, a positive purpose helps keep them engaged in a task and move towards a beneficial direction. My own involvement in martial arts took me away from negative behavior and led me towards profound understandings that assisted me later in my adult life. As mentors, the more we offer children these types of positive options and activities, the better. If a young person is engaged in a hobby, a sport or a positive activity; it will deter him/her from jeopardizing the thing they enjoy most.

For a young person, nothing is more critical than discovering their true potential. Once that confidence is there it helps provide a sense of self-direction that is truly invaluable.

CHAPTER 1 FOCUS

The first step on the *Journey to the Mountain Within* is towards the Mentorship. These are the relentless parents, neighbors, teachers, counselors, social workers, probation and law enforcement officers who reach out and provide guidance at crucial moments in a child's life. Together they provide a network of support. This support is crucial in the healthy development of teens that are in need of the *power of mentoring*. Mentoring builds character, leadership, and community enrichment.

CHAPTER II

THE SYSTEM

WHEN I WAS AN adolescent growing up in National City I would hear horror stories about friends and relatives who did time in youth correctional facilities. I heard these stories on street corners far from adult ears. My friends would often brag about how they survived incarceration, what they experienced, and what they saw someone else go through. I felt this type of communication among us was an unconscious form of preparation. It was as if hearing about it meant I was destined to be sent to a youth correctional facility.

Dad's wake-up call

I clearly remember a time in my early teens, when my brother Carlos and I wanted to play baseball with the kids in our neighborhood, but realized we had nothing to use as bases. It was an early summer evening in my neighborhood and the energy of families, either getting home from work or sitting down at dinner, buzzed throughout the air. You could hear the laughter of children racing their shabby second-hand bikes all over our neighborhood and almost everyone on our block was busy doing something.

Carlos and I were busy thinking of a plan to find baseball bases so we could play ball. Kimball Elementary School was two blocks from our house. We remembered that the school had durable mats that were kept under the monkey bars to prevent kids from being hurt when they fell. We decided to take those mats and use them for our game. While we took the mats from the school's property, my brother and I thought very little about what we were doing, knowing it was wrong. Instead, we imagined the fun we would have playing baseball on our street with real baseball bases.

Unfortunately, the police were waiting patiently outside the school gate as we walked out with the stolen mats under our arms. Their flashlights beamed into our faces, burning into our eyes and we froze like scared animals. I remember that in that moment the feeling of being caught doing something wrong took over. Carlos and I were placed inside the police car as we were escorted to the National City Police Department Station.

One of the officers wrote a police report about the incident and asked us many questions. We sat in an empty, cold room for what seemed to be a lifetime. The police officers talked to each other about sending my brother and me to that frightening place, Juvenile Hall. We were frightened and didn't know what to expect. The officers made it clear that we were not permitted to speak to each other. We waited for what seemed an eternity, in silence.

Fortunately, when my parents arrived at the police station, they recognized one of the sergeants who attended church with them.

Once they recognized my father, the police officers changed their attitude. They treated my father as a respected member of the community and kindly released us to him.

I have always wondered what my father said to the officers as he rescued us from the mess we put ourselves into. I also realize that our lives might have continued down a wrong path had my father not been the man he was.

The ride home was only a mile, but it seemed as though time stood still. I remember the hum of the car and the loud uncomfortable silence coming from my parents in the front seats.

My dad never had a problem scolding us or giving us a lecture about improper behavior. But on this occasion, after we were released from the police station he did not yell, lecture, hit us, or even send us to our room for the night. He never said a word about the incident. I think the situation scared him. The idea of his two sons being caught doing something wrong and ending up in the system shook him to the core. I saw fear on my father's face that night. For the first time, he realized that he could not control our actions or watch us all the time.

Many kids in my neighborhood did not have a father like mine. Too many suffered with fathers who where alcoholics, abusive, or absent. I was fortunate in that I had one who cared about me and my future. As I grew up, I participated in activities that could have sent me to jail, but I was fortunate not to experience that side of life. I look back and know that it was because I had a strong support system within my family, and a few extra guardian angels watching over me

Many of my friends and relatives did not have my same good fortune. Several of them went through the juvenile county facilities, and eventually graduated into the adult prison system.

Growing Pains

I went to elementary, middle, and part of high school with Ricardo. He was a handsome Mexican-Filipino with curly black hair that he combed into an *Afro*. His parents were migrant farm workers in the Central Valley. He had a healthy sense of humor, was agile, athletic, and well-liked within our community. His family lived about a half mile from mine and his older brothers, José and Pablo, were close friends with my older cousin, Manuel. José was a phenomenal high school quarterback. He had a talented arm when throwing the football.

Ricardo and his brothers were always visiting or playing sports on our neighborhood streets or at the community park. I remember that on several occasions after a heavy rain, Ricardo and many other boys our age played football at the park in a muddy make-shift football field until the sun went down. We would walk home from the park, caked with mud, looking like swamp monsters.

In high school, Ricardo began spending more time with rougher boys. These young men were often in trouble in school for fighting, for their drug or alcohol use, they refused to attend school, and many more forms of defiant behavior. I got involved in the world of high school sports and martial arts while Ricardo began to spend his time with young men who became drop outs with nothing but too much time on their hands. We stopped socializing.

Although our worlds were separate, rumors often reached my family about how Ricardo and his friends were getting in trouble with the police. These associations, and his lifestyle, eventually landed him in state prison, charged with murder. The word on the street was that he didn't commit the murder, but was not about to say who did. For Ricardo, *ratting out* to the judge was not an option. Consequently, while most teenagers were thinking about high school football games, parties and making plans for their future, Ricardo at eighteen was in a state prison with a twenty-five to life sentence.

I was aware he had been spending time with a dangerous crowd before going to prison, but I also knew he was not a bad person. He just got mixed up with the wrong crowd. I can only imagine what he went through in prison. At the age of nineteen, Ricardo was murdered in his single cell in San Quentin State Prison. Official prison reports state, that he died of strangulation and was found with a pillow over his head. A lot of people who knew Ricardo had a difficult time accepting his abrupt passing; he was much too young.

Stories like these were too common in my community. Many of my relatives and friends ended up in the county jail, and quite a few did time in prison. I often wondered about the statistics, why young men of color are more likely to get arrested and sent to a state prison than young men in more integrated, affluent communities.

Working in Probation

I grew up knowing that my mother wanted to work with young men and women to create positive change. But unfortunately, a lack of resources and the responsibility of raising a large family prevented her from pursuing that challenge. At twenty-three, I was given the opportunity to begin working for the Orange County Probation Department. From my first day on the job, I was motivated and felt I was going to accomplish something of value. Elated to have the opportunity my mother never had, I knew I was where I was supposed to be.

This was a career that promised to be aligned with my purpose, and helping youth made me feel incredibly fulfilled. I was enthusiastic and focused; I quickly learned how the Orange County Juvenile System was structured. I learned that the majority of the kids at Juvenile Hall were waiting to receive their sentencing from the court or to be transferred to other facilities. At that time, there were approximately 350 youth in detention/program units in Orange County.

Detention Units are for youth who have a short time to serve or are waiting to get their commitment sentence from the court or who are about to be transferred to either a probation camp, California Youth Authority or the County Jail. Program units were designed for the youth who had longer sentences and needed closer supervision. At the Orange County Juvenile Hall, the Program Units were isolated from the Detention Units. Program Units were for the youth who were older and much more criminally sophisticated.

I had to be alert with the Program Units; working with them was like searching for landmines. Some days, they were calm and focused on their daily activities. Other times, in blink of an eye, a violent fight would break out. Apart from the regular physical altercations, there were occasional attacks against staff by youth who were attempting to escape. I could never relax; I never knew what to expect. There were too many individuals with high levels of anxiety in one congested area. I knew better than to let my guard down.

Often all units were overcrowded, especially during the summer months, with as many as thirty youth occupying a space designed for twenty. Anyone who walked down that long hallway saw everything. We had to constantly supervise their showering or toilet use because many violent assaults were attempted in unsupervised areas. Two or three staff members supervised each unit. A control desk in each area was in communication with the main control area that oversaw the entire facility and responded to disruptions. Privacy was the one thing that did not exist in juvenile hall.

Dealing with Cultural Tension

Working in the facility was stressful. It did not help that I was one of the few Chicano staff members there. I could count all of us on one hand. Since the majority of the youth in custody were Latino, the staff who did not know me often had me mistaken for an inmate. I remember one deputy asking his co-worker, "What is that guy doing out of his room?" I guess most of the staff was not accustomed to Chicanos working with them at their level. I dealt with numerous cultural biases from my co-workers. I did not blame them for their ignorance; I blamed the lack of information that was available to them and their unwillingness to seek it out.

One day, my co-worker attempted to compliment me by telling me in a praising tone, "Hey, Louie. You know what you are? You are like a White Mexican." When I asked him what he meant, he responded: "Yeah Louie, it is because you are smart, you're great at communicating, and you're different from the other Mexicans I know."

At that time, working in Orange County, they didn't know what to do with me. Nothing could have insulted me more.

I believe that the root of any form of racism is ignorance and the best way to eradicate it is to have a healthy dialogue. I had an hour-long conversation with my well-intentioned co-worker in which I explained why his remark was not a compliment. I continued to have many more conversations with fellow co-workers about culture. Many of them were open and interested but there were those who were stuck in their limited thinking and indifferent.

Regardless of the drama that was part of my new job, I enjoyed it and knew I carried a responsibility to improve my work environment. I knew I was destined to learn and experience something there, although it was difficult to put into words. I understood I would have an opportunity to do something constructive in that environment. I worked long hours and volunteered for frequent extra shifts that came along. In those first seven years I received great evaluations and a lot of praise for my efforts from my superiors and colleagues.

On one occasion, I responded to a call on my radio to pursue a known Latino gang youth who was attempting to escape from the facility. He had managed to climb over the high fence. I was in the immediate area and volunteered to stop him. I chased him, running at a race pace for two miles through the Santa Ana Riverbed until he was gasping for air and too exhausted to try anything. While on his knees and holding his cramping stomach, the young man told me between his gasps for air, "I think I made you a hero. Man, you could run. Aren't you tired?" he asked.

I escorted the young man back to the booking area. He was not upset with me. He knew I was just doing my job. Whenever he would see me after his attempted escape, he would greet me respectfully even though he had received an extended sentence for his attempt.

At each facility, I wore many hats. Some days, I would pursue the minors who were attempting to escape, assisted in breaking up fights or riots, and counseled youth who were suicidal. I calmed inmates who were violently out of control and dealt with the youth who tried to physically harm me. Many were angry and had nothing to lose, a very dangerous combination. Often they would attempt to provoke me to fight. All I could do was remind them of how there was no victory when a person fought for nothing other than for the sake of fighting. I appealed to their logic, sense of morality and self-respect; most of the time it worked. I connected to them as human beings, not objects of the juvenile justice system.

Working in Probation

The staff came from all over the United States. Most people who worked in the probation department were young, college educated, talented, and energetic. One Deputy Probation Counselor was a champion who ran the 800 meter in the 1984 Olympic trials. And there were many guys who had careers in college basketball and football. While some were using the job as a stepping stone to bigger and better career opportunities, others were genuinely concerned about youth in custody and devoted their careers to helping the underprivileged.

These exceptional noble people, who worked at the correctional facilities had strong principles and values; a blessing to everyone. There were extremely talented counselors who were magically effective in their counseling abilities and were able to approach any troubled youth with a wide heart and open mind. Many of the staff had a solid spiritual foundation and some were outstanding in the way they connected with youth. I believe wherever they are today, they are adding to this world, touching the lives of numerous young people.

However, as my career continued in probation, I became frustrated. I learned that even with such amazing people working to help these incarcerated youth, there was still a high rate of recidivism and was determined to find out why.

First Impressions

One of the valuable lessons I learned in my job was that young people took about five minutes to assess the staff members they had to deal with - who was fair, who was mean, who was a push-over, and most importantly, who was a *burn-out*. By evaluating the person in charge they immediately were able to size-up how much they could get away with while in custody. On the streets, as well, it will take a youth seconds to evaluate the demeanor of a law enforcement officer.

For any future mentors, this is why the first five minutes you work with people are critical because that is when you set up boundaries and respect. If these boundaries are not established immediately, it is difficult to establish them later. In my career, I have found this rule to be applicable in many situations. The key is to use this rule to your advantage, to make your work easier, and better serve the people who need us most.

Negative Attitudes toward Incarcerated Youth

Many employees who are *burned-out* will release their frustrations on the job. *Burnout* has to do with one's inner attitude. If individuals are unhappy with their surroundings or feel stuck in an environment that no longer fulfills their needs, it has a profound impact on their motivation. When a person is *burned-out*, it is difficult for them to be able to do their job well. This lack of enthusiasm will

31

have an effect on their work and their interaction with people. It seemed that the employees who lost sight of why they were there were the most harsh and least empathetic. This attitude negatively affects incarcerated youth.

I began to observe this attitude in many people I worked with at various facilities. I did not know which was more dangerous: the angry youth, or the angry employees watching over them. To me, the youth had an obvious excuse for their anger; they were incarcerated. The adults were well-paid county employees. There seemed to be a consensus among some probation staff that they were better than the incarcerated youth. They would easily turn against the wards, or treat them in a dehumanizing manner.

Sometimes these efforts were subtle, sometimes cruelly obvious. Such feelings of superiority created not just a negative attitude toward the youth, but also a negative work environment for all of us. Perhaps this negative attitude made the job easier, helping staff to distract themselves from a feeling of disappointment in their own careers or in their personal lives. In any case, such an unproductive attitude did nothing in terms of reaching out to the youth inside.

Not to justify their actions, but I can say I now understand why some people got involved in criminal activity. Having grown up in a tough part of San Diego, I knew poverty and saw how easy it was to slip into that way of life. I had family on both sides of the law, but I never felt inferior or ashamed of the ones who were punished by society for their wrongdoing. Despite their actions, I knew their spirits were decent. I knew they merely had to pay a price for their bad choices.

Facilitating Programs

For many years I supervised the drug and alcohol programs at the Youth Guidance Center in Santa Ana, California. I networked with drug and alcohol agencies within the community and learned that many of these organizations were eager to work with youth. It was during this time in my career that I developed a gang intervention program for Latino youth. I tried to emphasize cultural pride as a means of raising self-esteem among the individual but also among parents and the community.

The program was great, but something was missing. Many of the youth continued to return, which meant the program's success rate was not what I had in mind.

I don't think the program had structural problems, these young men and women were so far along in gang activity that the program came too late in their lives to effect change. An intervention program is designed to help individuals make choices, but these kids were too deeply rooted in gang mentality. I tried to get the program to run effectively, but that wasn't enough.

Disillusionment with the system

After ten years of service, something happened to me: I felt *burned-out*. As the years passed I noticed the job draining me more and more. I came into work one day during my afternoon shift and the entire camp was on lockdown, meaning the youth were confined to their bunks for a day-and-a-half, due to their behavior. Since it was a large dorm room with over eighty beds, every noise or outburst was out in the open for everyone to witness. During lockdown, the youth are not permitted to talk, participate in outside or inside activities, and use of the phones.

The reason for this disruption involved two rival gangs who were about to *go to war*. Since I had a relationship with the leaders of both gangs, my superiors asked me to negotiate and prevent the potential riot. My bosses promised that they would continue to be on lockdown if the gangs did not resolve their conflict. I did not want them to fight; such riots were violent and often deadly. I spoke with both gang leaders separately. They each agreed not to fight within the institution.

One of the youth leaders agreed to remain peaceful if I would do something for him. He wanted me to promise him that they would be taken off lockdown if things remained calm. He asked me to give him my word, and I did without hesitation. The threat of them fighting was the only reason they were on lockdown in the first place. I told them they would be off lockdown by morning. Then, I wrote my report and gave it to my supervisors.

The environment became tranquil and hopeful within hours of my conversation with the gang leaders. While it was true the rival gangs could not stand each other, the fact was they were tired of staring at the ceiling from their beds, with no privileges. They were willing to call truce for a bit more freedom.

The next day during my afternoon shift, I was expecting the camp to be back to normal, but apparently, they were still on lockdown. Once I was spotted, one of the gang members stood up from his lower bunk bed and with a disgusted look, he called out to me, "Hey Man! You gave us your word!" Another young man yelled out the same. I heard one of the staff across the dorm tell them to shut up and get back to their bunks. The tension in the air was overwhelming.

I went straight into the administration office and asked my superiors what had happened. I knew how hard it was to build relationships with these young men. I also knew that once their trust was broken, how it was virtually impossible to get it back. I was upset and tried my best not to show my anger. I asked my supervisor, "Why weren't they taken off lockdown? I gave my word to those young men! I told them they would come off this structure if they promised not to fight."

I knew my supervisor could care less about what my character and integrity meant to these young men. He answered, nonchalantly, "I changed my mind. I don't trust these guys. They need to learn a lesson here. They don't run this place."

"You killed my credibility with them. I gave them my word." I explained.

"They'll get over it," he responded.

From that day forward I could not hide my frustration from my superiors. I could not accept the widespread attitude that it didn't matter if we kept our word because of who we were dealing with. The inmates were still people. They still deserved respect if they were willing to be respectful. I was no longer sure if I was being asked to be a counselor or a jail keeper, and I did not like the way the youth were being treated.

After that day, my heart was no longer in my job. I went from being a highly motivated employee to someone who was defiant and distrustful towards my work. At one point, I felt incarcerated in my job; I felt stuck. It was no longer about making a difference or moving up the career ladder of success. Something inside me just stopped believing that I had the power to impact change and make a difference with these kids. I knew that the people above me had the power to stop my efforts at any time.

The way I saw it, the system was like a dysfunctional family, one that blamed everyone else for its problems. Every year, we would be assigned more and more paper work, and most of it was based on covering the probation department from the growing pile of potential lawsuits. I began to steadily lose my focus, and I became disillusioned with my job.

Resignation: a Forced Decision

Two events finally forced me to make decision to end my career with Orange County Youth Correctional Facilities. The first had to do with Eduardo, a slim sixteen year old Chicano gang member from Santa Ana. I first met him when he tried to escape from Joplin Youth Center, a youth correctional camp. Since I was a well developed runner at the time, I was instructed to bring him back. Escaping from any probation facility was a serious offense. The minors usually received a minimum of thirty additional days for trying to flee from a probation facility.

I can still remember the pounding in my chest as I chased Eduardo down our main hill. I had only a county radio to communicate with my co-workers. I was slowly catching up to him and he was running like a high-speed jackrabbit. During the pursuit, as I was getting closer, I called out to him, "Eduardo you better stop! I am catching up! You'd better stop before you get hurt!"

He responded by saying in Spanish slang, "*Chale (No way)*! I ain't stopping!" I was able to see a serious determined look on his face. After the quick dialogue, he slid for six feet like a bad baseball slide on the paved slope 200 hundred feet from the front gate of the camp. I heard the snap. He had broken his leg. I immediately called for assistance to take him back to get medical attention. Eduardo was sent to the hospital.

A month after he returned, he was placed on my caseload. At the time, I was given the impression he was not too happy about that. From his perspective, I was the guy who prevented him from a victorious escape and the person responsible for his broken leg. I believe he spent almost a year with me. Within that year, he did a lot of growing-up. He changed his behavior and attitude. I began looking at his future from a different perspective. We spent countless hours discussing his life and future plans. He began to trust me and he confided in me that he did not want to live the life of a gang member. Eduardo wanted a normal life, free of violence. He became one of the youth leaders and had moved up the ranks in the Behavioral Modification Model of positive reinforcement. Within that time period I developed a level of trust with him.

Eventually, Eduardo was released after he completed his commitment. Six months later I got a call from a public defender.

He informed me that Eduardo had gone to Mexico and had not reported to his field probation officer for six months. When Eduardo returned to the United States he was subsequently arrested and placed into custody. His public defender wanted me and another co-worker to testify as character witnesses.

Character Witness

Eduardo's public defender informed us that his present probation officer was recommending nine years in the California Youth Authority (youth prison), often referred to as a "gladiator school". They housed youth up to the age of twenty-five at the time. According to several youth I have mentored that did time in CYA, the environment was violent and young men wanted to build reputations that would follow them to an adult state prison. To develop this reputation they had to hold their own in fights, racial riots, and not allow others to take advantage of them.

To this day, I do not agree with the recommendation. I thought it was excessive and pointless. The prevailing philosophy was that the best way to deal with gang members was to put them away for long periods of time; that was the solution. But it just did not make sense to me. The probation officer and district attorney involved in this case did not know Eduardo; they never saw the great changes he had initiated. I knew my testimony on Eduardo's behalf was going to create conflict with my supervisors and directors.

A day before going to court, one of the administrators of Joplin Youth Center called me into his office to prepare my testimony.

He explained that I was not qualified to make a recommenda-tion on the minor's behalf because I was only a Deputy Probation Counselor. I asked him for his recommendations and he told me to say something to the effect that: *I should let others that are more qualified make that decision.* He also stated that I was not quali-fied to suggest what outcomes would be best for Eduardo, "Let them know that you are not qualified to make that decision."

Sarcastically I asked, "Do you want me to lie? Aren't I sup-posed to tell the truth?"

He paused as he heard my remark. And in a threatening tone said, "Be careful, Ruan."

I decided to testify along with another co-worker. Since I wasn't present in the court when she took the stand I don't know what she told the court. Then it was my turn. I already knew what I was going to say. While on the stand in Juvenile Court, I saw Eduardo and his family. Eduardo smiled at me. I also saw a probation administrator in the public area. He was taking notes; he never made eye contact with me.

After a series of questions, the public defender asked me the big question, "How much time should Eduardo receive?" I sat there looking at the judge and then I looked across at the probation official.

I took a deep breath and told the court that I felt that Eduardo would not benefit from an extensive sentence in the California Youth Authority, that such a sentence would only make matters worse. He would become more criminally sophisticated and a heavier burden on society overall. I had Eduardo on my caseload for more than a year, and I felt I knew his positive potential. He needed counseling for drug abuse, family counseling, and job training. I told them I thought the fact he was a registered gang member who had gone to Mexico without the consent of his probation officer did not warrant a prolonged incarceration of nine years.

As a result of my testimony, Eduardo received less than a year for his case. I was not able to see him because of strict probation policies, but his lawyer shared the promising news with me. I felt I did the right thing, but I knew I was going to pay a price for it.

A few days after court, a co-worker of mine, working a night shift, was snooping in the director's office. He found a memo from another administrator that was about me. The memo read something to the effect that during Eduardo's hearing I was unprofessional, poorly dressed, had messy long hair and looked as if I came to court after a five-day drinking binge.

None of it was true. I had been dressed for court. I wore a sports coat, with a nice shirt and dress slacks. I was never much of a drinker, and I did not drink the night before. I probably looked tired because I was tired. I worked crazy hours, and I was also stressed out thinking about Eduardo's case and my testimony.

I felt the remarks in the memo were vindictive, hurtful, and unprofessional: *out-of-line*. When I received this information I was upset and wanted to put that arrogant administrator in his place. I requested my director open an investigation regarding the content of the memo and told him I wanted the administrator to receive consequences for slander and unprofessional behavior.

My director indicated that taking action against him would affect my ability for upward mobility, and that I should be careful. I told him that I was indifferent about moving up any career ladders.

I also told him how that administrator's actions were inappropriate and untrue. He knew I was upset. He said, "Okay. You want an investigation? I want the name of the person who gave you that memo. You give me his name, and we will have an investigation." He knew I would not give him the name. I told him I could not reveal my source. He responded by telling me that without the name, the investigation would cease.

After that incident, I became apathetic and more verbal about my views toward my work. By then, I was no longer anyone's favorite or the golden child. That incident left me with a bitter taste, and it reinforced my resentment toward the probation department.

Last Incident

What happened next made my decision to leave my job, easier. I was supervising a group of young men at one of the Juvenile Correctional Camps. We were cleaning a shed near several large trash bins. I had the minors working on the road and in the trash shed sweeping, cleaning, hosing down, and pulling weeds. One of my co-workers drove up before his shift, and asked me for an update of the group.

After he drove away, I immediately noticed that one of the young men had a large cut around his eye and was bleeding profusely. I gave him my T-shirt to stop the bleeding. Whenever something of that nature occurs, it is procedure to escort all the minors back into their areas, place them on lockdown, and begin the investigation. The minor who was injured at first told me he had an accident; he was raking and injured his eye when he tripped and accidently rammed the rake near his eye.

After questioning more minors, I discovered what really happened. He had been in a fight with another minor that resulted in him getting a flashy black eye. To avoid getting in trouble for fighting, he rammed the rake into his eye to make the whole thing seem like an accident. Fighting in a probation facility results in doing more time, so often, the youth try to fabricate what happened to avoid serious consequences. I completed the investigation and submitted the information to my supervisor.

Much to my surprise several days later, my supervisor told me that the administration had decided to conduct an investigation for my participation in the incident, due to what they felt was my poor supervision. I knew it was because they wanted to get rid of me because of my past remarks. In a facility such as this one, fights and violence were very common. Investigations regarding staff hardly ever happened. I felt targeted.

My supervisor asked me if I wanted a union representative during the investigation; they were going to read me my peace officer rights. This was very serious. In my ten years in the department, I had never had my rights read to me.

At that point in my probation career, I was tired and disgusted with the entire system and had become a cynical and a *burned-out* employee. I became part of what I had never wanted to become. After talking to my wife and reflecting on the situation, I decided to quit the probation department once and for all. I couldn't stomach being in a place that I despised. It wasn't the youth inside the facility, what sickened me was the hypocrisy and dysfunction of the people running the place.

I went into the investigation meeting and the administrators all sat around with their legal papers, a copy of the peace officer rights, and a tape recorder to capture my responses. I asked the individuals around me if I could make a statement. They nodded.

"After much thought, I have decided that it would be the best decision if I resigned from the probation department. Here is my written letter of resignation. I would like to resign in two weeks." They looked at me in disbelief. Their goal had been to use my job as a carrot to dangle in front of me, to intimidate me. They never anticipated I would make such a decision.

Consequently, I resigned from my position as Deputy Probation Counselor. I felt as if I was leaving a bad marriage; I was being released from my own prison. I knew it was a stable and secure job, but I just could not stomach it anymore.

That all happened in the fall of 1995; I just had had enough. I was the epitome of a *burned-out* county employee. I did not believe in my work anymore. I knew I should have resigned years earlier, but I always felt as if things would improve and that I could make a difference in the lives of the youth I was dedicated to serve.

Struggling with my career, I started to look for options outside of the system. I had started working with another group of at-risk youth outside the facility. After leaving the probation department, I realized that Juvenile Justice System was not an effective solution to redirecting criminal behavior. It was an ineffective approach that created dependency and failed to address the core issues of the current challenges that youth faced.

CHAPTER 2 FOCUS

Understanding the problem that permeates youth violence is an encouraging step towards creating viable healing solutions in today's world. It is imperative to research, assess, and to thoroughly study the core issues that motivate youth violence. This gathered specialized information will provide direction and assist in developing a successful approach. Understanding the problem is the foundation of creating an effective and comprehensive perspective in dealing with youth issues.

CHAPTER III

FIRST EXCURSION

I RECALL AN EXPERIENCE WHILE in the Probation Department that reinforced my determination to work with teens. I remember going to Juvenile Court in Orange County to support a family who had asked for my help. Their son had a court date to terminate his probation. I waited outside the courtroom for the family thinking of how many courtroom hallways I have sat in throughout my career assisting Latino, Vietnamese, and African American youth and their families.

In this case, two public defenders emerged from a closed empty courtroom. The first said, "If your last name begins with A through L, I am your public defender, if your name begins with M to Z, then *she* is your attorney," pointing toward his colleague. "So please line-up with your attorney because court is going to begin in twenty minutes."

The young men lined up unsure of what their fate would be. I would say that most of those young men did not go home that afternoon, instead sent to Juvenile Hall for their crimes. What caught my attention was how these young people, many of them gang members and repeat offenders, were able to face their reality so easily. This had a profound effect on my perspective of the Juvenile Justice System. I could not help but wonder why incarceration had become the only alternative in dealing with youth issues. It was something that failed to shock the youth or scare them. They were so used to being institutionalized that they hardly responded when the judges tapped their gavels in judgment. Such scenes motivated me to find an alternative.

The *Beyond Limits Program* began. It was designed to be an opportunity to help young people who did not have financial resources, family support, or guidance to change their destructive lifestyles. It was important for me to work outside of this criminal justice system, an institutionalized process that preys on individuals who lack economic and social resources. I needed to find a way to work with them on my own terms.

Beyond Limits Vision

My vision was to develop a program that was accessible to urban at-risk youth and culturally youth-friendly. Traditionally, a program that was this unique and was able to bring forth positive change in young adults did not attract funding. This would be an intervention that would focus on kids who normally wouldn't have the economic and social resources to create the success they desired. I shared this vision with three men: Octavio Gonzalez, Miguel Bernal, and Mario Fuentes. They were instrumental in shaping *Beyond Limits* during the developing years of the program. The initial founders shared my dream of creating a program that would equip youth with the necessary tools to succeed in life.

We officially started the *Beyond Limits Program* in the spring of 1990 and became a 501c3 nonprofit program in 1991 (I was actively involved in *Beyond Limits* while employed for the Orange County Probation Department). The program did not accept money from alcohol or tobacco companies because of philosophical standards: the negative impact they had on communities of color. We depended on small grants and grassroots fundraising. While I was active in *Beyond Limits*, no one received a salary and it was entirely organized by community volunteers.

First Beyond Limits Excursion – Mt. Whitney

I decided to be more ambitious with this group of youth than I could be with the ones I worked with in probation and began to organize a backpacking excursion to Mt. Whitney. I held presentations at high schools, continuation schools, talked to neighborhood families – I wanted to be sure the kids I took with me wanted to change their lives. For the first time in a long time, I felt I was back on the right path. My heart began to feel full again.

The adults who took part in the first *Beyond Limits* excursion were friends of mine. There was Octavio Gonzalez, a co-worker/ friend in the probation department with a healthy sense of humor, Miguel Bernal a talented musician and friend, and George Morales a former gang member from the City of Santa Ana, who was a college student at the time. All three of these men volunteered and believed in the success of the program. For me, it was the first time I would be attempting something of this enormity, to backpack eighty-two miles in Mother Nature's backyard with three street-raised Latino youth.

After working with the youth for several months and building their trust, they were ready. We rented a van to take them out of their neighborhoods to see what else the world had to offer – we were on our way to Mt. Whitney. The plan was to begin the excursion at Crescent Meadow trailhead and backpack east to Mt. Whitney, a total of 82 miles to our pick up location at Whitney Portal trailhead. The excursion was over mountains from the west section of California Sequoia National Park to the furthest east section in Inyo National Forest.

After driving seven hours, we finally reached the Sequoia National Park in Central California. We arrived in time to set up camp, cook a quick meal, and get into our sleeping bags before midnight.

That first night, I intentionally camped apart from the group in an area where I had a perfect view of the evening stars. I wanted to be alone, to allow the beauty of the night sky to distract my thoughts of responsibility. But my distraction was short-lived; I remembered the reactions I received when I told others about my idea of taking a group of at-risk kids on a backpacking trip. The doubting voices wanted to know what changes this would do and if it would keep these kids out of jail: "Why do you want to take a bunch of troubled kids with you to the mountains? If you are not careful they will probably push you off the mountain, and then what will you do?"

This comment came from a friend who worked with in the probation department. These thoughts floated through my mind like clouds with no direction. I spent most of the night periodically waking up with different worries of what needed to be done the next day until my fatigue finally prevailed.

After a few hours of sleep, I was up strolling through the tranquil campsite during the early morning; everyone else was still sleeping. It was five in the morning and the early morning light was climbing up behind the mountains, preparing for the sun to make its grand entrance. I wandered from the campsite where I could be alone with my thoughts, the sting of cold air keeping me alert. As I strolled and stared at the towering sequoia trees, I began to feel the stress of being responsible for three young people as well as three adults.

A week before, four of the nine youth originally cleared to participate were in custody for probation violations, another youth was involved in a gang fight and was hospitalized, and the last one was not able to take part in the trip because he had a painful toothache that needed immediate attention.

There were remaining three young men who were cleared to attend the excursion. First there was Joe, sixteen and Latino, who worked evenings and weekends with his parents cleaning office buildings. He was having problems in school and on the verge of joining his neighborhood gang. Then there was Eddie, an easygoing young man with a pleasant smile who was in a court school for youth who have been kicked out of regular schools. And finally there was Peter, the type of kid that had leadership skills, but could also be very difficult to work with.

My goal was to hike to the summit of Mt. Whitney, the second highest mountain in the United States and take them with me. My intention was to provide, through the challenges of backpacking, a physical, mental, and spiritual metaphor of what is possible when one is focused and prepared. I wanted that image of accomplishment to remain in their memory, to help them through the hardships of life.

Despite my optimistic intentions, negative thoughts continued to rush through my head. "You're crazy for doing this! What if somebody gets a serious injury? Can I really lead this group almost eighty-two miles over the summit of Mt. Whitney?" I took a deep breath and reminded myself that everything was going to be fine. After all, my friends, George Morales, Octavio Gonzalez, Miguel Bernal, and I had spent six months planning every detail of this challenging excursion: how much food each person would need (not packing too much and not starving the youth), where we would get water, where we would camp, how many miles we would travel, obtaining permits to enter the national park and the forest service, gathering weather reports, and making sure the youth were in decent physical condition. I wanted these three young men, these potential gang members, to have the best possible experience. I wanted them to look at life differently, to take them to the top of a mountain to become aware that there was a *summit of their potential.*

Camping with Youth

The teenagers preferred to sleep all together in one cheap, beat-up army tent. After prodding him a bit the night before, Eddie secretly confided how they were scared to sleep out in the open, like the adults. I found it ironic how sensitive they were on the inside while they tried to be tough on the outside.

The next morning, after I woke up the three adult volunteers, I walked over to where the three young men were sleeping. I shook the tent, but earned no response. In my best motivated tone I said, "All right gentleman, it is time to get up!" Peter, eager to make a name throughout the gang world, responded with a rude, immature attitude, "Who in the fuck is making all the fucking noise!" His obscene language didn't match the scenic beauty around us. I cut him off immediately.

"Good morning to you. Now get up! I want all of you ready. Your mama isn't here to do everything for you. We need to get going within the hour." There was silence. Then, I could hear Peter mumble inappropriate remarks to the others. As I walked away, I realized figuring out how we would climb Mt. Whitney was definitely not the only challenge ahead of us: Peter's entire family was involved in gang culture.

Beginning the Journey

Once the boys were up and ready, we ate breakfast and prepared our backpacks for our first day of hiking. On the trailhead at Crescent Meadow, the adults said a quick prayer and reminded everyone where to re-group for lunch. For better supervision and safety, an adult was situated in the front and an adult at the end of each line. In those days I was in great physical condition I chose to be the lead in our group. Sometimes the group was miles from each other but nobody passed up the lead person or walked behind the pick-up person (the individual at the end of the line). The adult hiking in front of everyone had to be willing to walk at a fast pace and had to pay close attention to the trail. If the lead person became lost, everyone would be lost.

That first day, we hiked a strenuous eleven miles to the Bearpaw Campsite where black bears were said to frequent the area. After hiking all day, the last part of the trail, the last mile, was the most difficult. It had a steep incline that led to the campsite. Once we arrived, we had to secure our food in our sleeping bag pouches, tie them to inaccessible high tree branches, or secure the food in metal bear lockers that were used to keep the bears away from meals and supplies.

The hike up to the Bearpaw Campsite with our full backpacks became physically demanding. Our backs and leg muscles were sore and we were pushed to the limit. Most of the youth did not eat that evening; they just set up their tents and went to bed. Peter managed to stay up and irritate the ones who were trying to sleep with his boasting of gang fights. He was beginning to annoy everyone so I told him to go to sleep.

"You adults are bossy!" he said in a frustrated tone.

"Good night!" Octavio and Miguel echoed with a tone of impatience.

The next day the goal was to hike half the distance we did the previous day to Hamilton Lakes. The youth were lethargic the next morning because of the previous day's physical demands. This resulted in them being slow to get ready and organize their backpacks.

Once we were moving, the pace of the entire excursion was going to be physically, mentally, and emotionally demanding, and these youth were not accustomed to this form of intensity. Each morning we washed up, cooked, organized our backpacks, and cleaned our area. The group had to be ready to hit the trail by 8 a.m. Once out, we hiked all day in the bright sun with our 40/50 pound backpacks. During lunch we would take an hour break to rest or eat.

Throughout the entire journey the three volunteers and I worked to constantly offer positive reinforcement among our young hikers. We needed to build a sense of discipline, attentiveness, and group responsibility in order for the adventure to teach them anything. It had to be clear that everyone had to work as a team if the group was to reach our destination, safely and successfully.

Backpacking Philosophy

Another philosophy we shared with the youth was to preserve and respect the land. We reminded them to take only pictures and leave only foot prints. We did not take anything from the land and we did not leave any trash while hiking. The message we wanted to show the youth was that we had to do our part to preserve the land. The only two who complained were Peter and Joe. They really did not like the idea of preserving the land and were indifferent about the values we were teaching. Peter and Joe saw it as though we were being too demanding and were getting in the way of their fun.

During one of my discussions, Peter made it clear that he did not enjoy the adults correcting his behavior and he did not like the fact that he had to depend on us to survive. I just smiled at Peter and asked him to trust us and to relax. He would just nod his head with a defiant and distrustful look on his face and walk away. Eddie did not always get involved in Peter's drama; he was easier to deal with and had a better attitude. Eddie was a good-natured young man, but during his vulnerable moments, he would sometimes get pulled into Peter's negativity.

As we began our trek out of the Bearpaw Campsite area, we could see the glaciated peaks of the Great Western Divide in the distance. I wanted the group to take their time reaching the Hamilton Lake, to give them an opportunity to enjoy the alluring, lush scenery. I wanted them to take in how we were in an area that was absent of roads, helicopters, traffic noise, televisions or radios. After all, this was something unlike anything any of them had ever seen before.

On the way to our campsite we hiked near a scenic waterfall. We stopped and had lunch. From where we were, the view of the Sequoia National Park was breathtaking, extending far beyond the vista. The group seemed relaxed and content to be surrounded by nature's majestic perfection. After lunch, we hiked a few more miles to Hamilton Lake and set up camp thirty feet from the lake. Fortunately, we were the only group in the campsite. The young men explored the area and had time to be kids. Once we were settled, we enjoyed a nice dinner and planned the next day. The group slept near the lake with a spectacular view of Hamilton Lake and the towering Kaweah Mountain pass which we would hike the next day.

The moon's reflection upon the water gave the gray and white granite of the Kaweah Gap an illustration of nature's natural power. From my sleeping area, I had the best view of the stars, and I could see the abundance glittering throughout the evening sky. I enjoyed a perfect view from the comfort of my sleeping bag. I had a feeling of gratitude and inner peace that evening. That night I went into a profound and silent sleep.

The next day we were on the trail by 7:30 a.m. to be prepared for the physical and mental challenge of the hike. There was nowhere to go but up, with most of the trail being over the mountain. From a distance, the hike was intimidating for the novice backpacker and we wanted to give the youth ample time to safely hike over the Kaweah Gap. The adults remained close to the young men on that trail in order to avoid any potential accidents.

We arrived at the top of Eagle Scout Peak, 10,700 ft., at around noon. We were surrounded by patches of snow and a half-frozen Precipice Lake that had a series of shallow glacier ponds adjacent to most of the trail. From that point on, it was all a downhill hike to the Big Arroyo campground. We hiked a total of fifteen arduous miles that day to the campsite. That evening we set up camp, cooked, made plans for the next day, and went to sleep early. Everyone was exhausted and a bit cranky.

Joe had a short fuse that evening. He was irritable and his negative behavior was displayed through complaints about the hike and the food. Later, I believe Octavio and George spoke with him and helped get his attitude on track. I knew he missed his family. Being in the middle of the Sierra Nevada mountain range, away from family and the comforts of home, can be taxing to the mind and can hinder the ability to focus on the trip. We tried our best to be understanding and to give him his space.

The following morning, our goal was to hike to the Kern River Campsite. The day began at 6 a.m., and we were on the trail within the hour for a full day of backpacking through challenging terrain. The guys lacked motivation that morning. They were not used to the intense physical pace and discipline. They went through the motions and soon were on the trail. While hiking, they looked like zombies, the kind who dragged their physical bodies to a destination but who had their minds somewhere else. For these young men their thoughts were still about sleeping and waking up without any adults to remind them of what to do.

The last portion of the hike was along the Kern River where our campsite had a natural hot spring adjacent to the river. The team arrived at our designated campsite after completing an exhausting fifteen mile hike. The group was only four days away from our goal of reaching the summit of Mt. Whitney and we were beginning to feel the physical and emotional strain of backpacking in the remote Sierra Nevada backcountry. I could see it in everyone's attitude, especially the youth who were so obviously way out of their element.

In one movement, I took my 50-pound backpack off and placed it against a rock about three feet high. I then took off my overworked boots and rested my back on the softness of my backpack. Walking since early morning, and then the heat had taken a lot out of me. My legs were sore and wobbly like rubber, feeling as if I had just run a marathon. I began to close my eyes and drift off. One of the finer experiences of backpacking is being able to rest and re-energize in nature.

Conflicts on the Trail

My nap was quickly interrupted by one of the adults yelling out to me, "Louie, Louie! We need your help, two of the guys are about to fight!" I struggled to put on my boots and jumped up fast as I could, half asleep and untied shoe laces.

I wedged myself between the two: "Hey guys, what's happening? What's the problem?"

The fight was between Peter and Eddie. I had noticed they had been verbally provoking each other from the beginning of the trip.

Their attitudes, combined with fatigue, had resulted in escalated conflict.

I asked the guys to sit down, staring at each other like two street pit bulls about to launch their best attack. I barked at them again, "Sit down, now!" I was starting to get upset. They slowly responded and took their time. Once they appeared to calm down, I asked why they wanted to fight each other.

Peter said, "Eddie is a punk and he talks a lot of shit!"

Eddie responded with a barrage of street Chicano slang and obscenities. Because of the beauty of our location, it bothered me how disrespectful they were acting. I was fed up and wanted this conflict ended. I said to them,

"Look! I am tired. I was just about to take a deep nap under a shady tree next to the river, and I am tired of the constant whining. If you guys want to fight, I think you should go for it…" They looked at me as if I were crazy. "Yeah, I think you guys should get it over with… I give you my permission." They both gave me a puzzled look.

Then came my condition, "If you do choose to fight, this is what is going to happen: If one of you gets a twisted ankle or dislocated elbow, remember we have a lot of miles of backpacking over steep mountains to complete. We have no hospitals or helicopters to pick you guys up. We are all alone here in the mountains. If one of you gets hurt, I am not going to help – you're on your own."

They looked at each other, and then Peter said, "I will kick his ass after the trip, when I get home."

Eddie responded, "You know where to find me, *pendejo!*" Having called Peter an "idiot" was a direct challenge. They walked off in opposite directions.

I remember that evening, Peter was arguing with Eddie about whose turn it was to put up the tent. Octavio approached Peter, saying to him, "You know what you need?" Octavio had a gift for diffusing tense situations with his quick humor.

Peter responded in a defensive manner, "What do I need?"

Octavio stepped close to him and embraced him like a father would embrace his son. "You need a hug, man." Octavio then embraced Peter. For the first time, Peter didn't have any smart, rude remarks. He accepted the hug and seemed to be more at ease that day. I realized how I was too busy being strict with Peter, that I forgot he was a kid who needed affection. That basic fatherly hug interrupted his aggressive rhythm.

That evening I was surprised by Peter's change of behavior. Before going to sleep, all of us took turns enjoying the natural hot spring and then cooling off in the lake that was a few feet away. The boys appeared to appreciate this part of the day. After a long day of hiking, the hot spring was effective in revitalizing their sore muscles and diffusing some of their stored-up anger.

The next day we were scheduled to hike ten miles to Junction Meadow and then up a mountain to Wallace Creek. The terrain was mostly flat, a welcomed break from the steep switch back trails we had hiked. Joe and Peter were beginning to get grouchy and did not want to continue. Their remarks only sounded like whining:

"Why can't we stay here and *kick it?*"

"I don't want to go any further now... I want to rest!"

"Why do we have to always listen to the adults... why can't we do what we want?"

Most of the remarks were coming from Joe and some from Peter; the physical and mental demands were getting to them. I said, "We have people meeting us at Whitney Portal to take us back home... these people have taken time from work to give us a ride and it would not be polite to have them wait an extra day because we are a little tired." By that time, I had to admit I was beginning to get tired and a bit irritable with these kids. My patience was wearing thin. Fortunately, Miguel and Octavio diffused the situation by offering guidance to Joe and Peter.

Thanks to the mentoring of my father, I had many backpacking experiences and had witnessed the breaking point during a demanding backpacking excursion when the physical, mental, and emotional strains are expressed in many forms. A break down can come out by having a tantrum, acting angry, shutting down, blaming others, or isolating oneself, to name a few. It is a common occurrence and requires a lot of patience; a natural reaction that shows us where our minds are. When people are uncomfortable with their environment, their mind goes into survival mode, and begins to play games and drive reason and stability to a negative unproductive path, the breaking point of an individual.

Conversations with Peter

To avoid outbursts and acts of frustration, it is important to always diffuse a volatile situation before it gets out of control. This is why, during the hike to Wallace Creek from Junction Meadow, I asked Peter to hike with me behind the entire group. By this point on the trip, he was on *everyone's last nerve*. He was clueless as to how he was affecting the group with his negative attitude. I wanted to use that day of hiking to take him away from everyone else and to have a productive conversation and realign his behavior.

Peter loved to argue. While he could at times, be annoying, he appeared to listen to me and respect my leadership. The trail we were on was straight up, on an incline. It was so steep that at every fifteen minutes, we had to stop and catch our breath. As we found a rock to rest on, Peter took off his backpack and sat there on a ledge overlooking a magnificent view, in deep thought.

He turned around to me and said, "All we do is go up and down mountains. This sucks! Sometimes I like you for bringing me on this trip; sometimes I hate you for bringing me."

By this time, I was used to his direct harshness. He stood over me waiting for an answer while I sat there, enjoying the spectacular view. "Climbing up this mountain is like life: difficult, full of obstacles, and beautiful at the same time. You could go up the mountain angry and with attitude, and go down the mountain with the same useless negative attitude. If you ask me, I think it is a waste of energy!" He sat there with a confused look. I couldn't tell if what I had said had hit him deeply or if he thought I was talking nonsense. "A better way of doing this is with a positive mental attitude and awareness."

"What do you mean?" he asked.

"See, when I go up a mountain, I pace myself. I hike at a pace that is at my level. I do not try to do too much and suffer for it later.

As I go up the mountain, I enjoy the many beautiful sites around me. I realize that each moment is sacred because it will not repeat itself."

He began to laugh. "Aren't you sensitive?"

I interrupted his sarcastic laugh by asking him, "Did you see the waterfall two miles down? How about the deer that was drinking water at the spring that was at the foot of the trail? How about the hawks that were soaring above us for the last two hours? I know you saw the bear tracks."

"No, Louie! I didn't see that stuff," he said in a confused tone.

"Like I said, you need to develop your awareness and a positive mental attitude. You give into your negative mind too easily. This negative mind blinds you from experiencing all the good things that surround you. Your negative mind will always betray you."

His response to my words was interesting. He kept trekking up the incline, but for the remainder of the day, he was surprisingly quiet. Perhaps he had heard me.

That afternoon, we hiked up to an area near Wallace Creek where Miguel had found a safe place to camp on the side of the mountain. By the time I arrived with Peter to the campsite, everybody was settled in and had set up camp. Miguel was feeling sick and was exhausted from hiking at a brisk pace up the mountain. He skipped dinner and went to bed early. He was in a bad mood and asked to be left alone. I realized the pressure, physical fatigue, and elevation had pushed his limits too. Respecting that, we left him alone.

It was almost the end of the sixth day, when I noticed Joe, Eddie, and Peter were establishing a mountaineering rhythm among themselves. Their bodies were stronger and they were more prepared to handle these mountains. They also started to be more self-sufficient. Without any adults nagging them, they did everything they had to do: setting up camp, cooking, starting a fire, cleaning up, and purifying their water, etc., without being reminded.

The following day we decided to have an easy hike to our next destination. We instructed everyone to take their time waking up and hiking to our next campsite. The young men were relieved of the pressure of waking up early or getting to a location before a specific time. For that hike, there was no point person or pick-up person. We all had the opportunity to arrive before sundown and just enjoy the day.

Changes in the Youth

The young men were the last ones to arrive back to camp that late afternoon. Joe and Eddie enjoyed catching fresh golden trout from the lake with George so much that they were willing to share one fishing pole. Peter took his time exploring the lake perimeter and searched for life beneath the ankle deep shallow water. The young men looked peaceful; it was displayed on their faces and in their demeanor.

That evening, we had an encouraging talk about the next day's hike. We agreed to wake up at 5 a.m. and get to the summit before the afternoon. As the sun went down, so did the temperature. It was the coldest evening we had experienced during the entire excursion. The bitter cold made it so I could not sleep comfortably.

The next day, it would take the six of us half a day to reach the summit, five miles of treacherous steep hiking, thin air, and unpredictable weather. After what felt like forever, we arrived at the summit before mid-day. We took pictures, embraced each other and marveled at the panoramic view from the highest point in the continental United States. I felt like I was on top of the world. "I am close to heaven," I thought. Standing on the mountain gave me a sense of how high I was from sea level. It was a mysterious and moving moment.

We had six more miles down the mountain to our campsite at Outpost camp. As we hiked down the mountain, I was overwhelmed by our accomplishment as a group. Once we were on the eastern face of the mountain, we saw a lot of hikers making their attempt to the summit. We had smiles on our faces knowing the most difficult part of our journey was behind us; their journey had just begun.

Peter spent most of the downhill trek with the adults; he was now calm and easier to talk to. The group arrived at Outpost Camp by 4 p.m. Everybody was in high spirits because we knew we were almost home. We had our last backpacking meal with the kids and then decided to have a *processing session* with the youth. We collected feedback and reinforced the positive teachings; everyone seemed eager to participate. Eddie and Joe were proud of what they had achieved and could not wait to go home and share their experiences. Surprisingly, Peter mentioned that he did not want to go home and said he was going to miss the mountains.

Nature, in its mysterious power, had had a serious impact on young Peter's life. He had matured in those mountains; something inside Peter had transformed. Perhaps he realized that there was more to life than how he had seen it before. I was so proud, happy that the trip impacted him the way I had hoped it would. Still defensive when I complimented Peter on his positive changes, his defensive response was, "What are you trying to say?" He had no idea how difficult he had been. I had to let him know, "You were a real pain in the butt from the beginning."

He immediately countered, "You staff is too strict with us!"

Miguel, in a fatherly manner, said: "You were difficult for most of the trip, and to be honest, I really did not like your attitude. I know this trip has been difficult for you, but your attitude was also challenging. But I am glad that you have made changes."

As Miguel finished, Peter had an expression on his face of complete surprise, again revealing he did not realize the effect his behavior had on others. He took it for granted that he was okay with everyone, that his way was the only way. Nobody had ever told him that his behavior was abrasive, or maybe this was the first time he was willing to listen.

The best learning occurs through actual involvement...
In retrospect, the excursion was a success and we all learned a lot from every aspect. We were all happy to have met the challenge and were eager to get home to our families. Fortunately, we were able to complete the trip without any injuries or accidents. The group successfully completed the Mount Whitney Challenge,

a monumental feat, something many can only dream about. It became metaphor, an example of what can be achieved through hard work, a positive mental attitude, and planning.

Sadly, over time, I lost touch with these young men. Some of them moved and were no longer in the same schools.

CHAPTER 3 FOCUS

Reaching the summit of a challenging mountain is a reference point of success and a manifestation of what is possible, a form of success that will never be forgotten. It is a reminder of what can happen if the youth prepare, work hard, and make smart choices. They need to perceive success with a concrete experience to accept it. Successes in wilderness programs are based on using natural challenges to bring out solid life skill lessons, that young people are able to utilize to live their potential. The achievement of difficult physical experiences opens the mind and heart to unseen opportunistic avenues.

CHAPTER IV

MY FATHER'S INFLUENCE

WHILE ON THE EXCURSIONS, the boys asked me how I learned to backpack. After all, such a thing was not considered a hobby by many from my neighborhood. Every time they asked, I thought of my father. He had taught me everything I know about what it takes to *backpack* a challenging mountain. My father had learned most of his survival skills while in the U.S. Army Infantry during World War II and valued nothing more than to be outdoors camping, fishing, or backpacking. I remember how he loved to tell us stories about his long arduous foot soldier hikes through battlegrounds in Norway and Germany. I remember a particular story he often shared with me...

His company was on an extended recognizance march. He had just received a brand new pair of leather G.I. boots and did not have time to break them in when his entire company was ordered to march to a specific location.

He marched for twenty miles with a full military backpack, an M-1 rifle, and brand new stiff leather combat boots. By the end of the day, his feet were throbbing with bloody, painful blisters. Since he could no longer walk, his superiors gave him an order to stay back by himself until his feet were healed.

During his recovery, he had obstacles to work through: he was in enemy territory and had to find a shelter where he could not be seen or heard. He spent many stressful, sleepless nights before managing to hike to the safety of his company at their location.

After two years of many more vigorous military operations that threatened his survival, my dad was honorably discharged as a sergeant. Because of his military experiences, he developed a deep love for anything that had to do with the outdoors.

Marriage and the birth of six children temporarily interrupted my father's connection with the great outdoors. As soon as we began to grow up, he was eager to share outdoor experiences with our family. As a young child I remember many camping trips to Baja California, Mexico, the San Diego Mountains, the Los Angeles Forest, as well as the Sierra Nevada Mountains. We would camp out in these areas with a large military green tent that held the entire family. My father made sure we had all the necessary camping equipment needed.

The last time I backpacked with my dad, I was fifteen, in the ninth grade and in superior physical condition from martial arts training and running for the track team at National Middle School. My father, my cousin Rey from Los Angeles, my younger brother Carlos, and I took part in a weekend backpacking trip in the Cleveland National Forest in the San Diego County Mountains.

During this excursion, my father hiked at a slow pace. I noticed that he was getting older and was not as strong as he once was. My brother and I hiked alongside him throughout most of the trip. I was able to spend quality time with my dad, a quiet man; it was enjoyable to be with him in his favorite environment.

I also have fond memories of family beach gatherings. I remember watching my dad, a few hours before sundown, bring out his favorite deep sea fishing pole. Living in San Diego County, near the ocean, we had countless beach barbeques with *carne asada*, with extended family and friends. While everyone else was busy eating or participating in beach activities, my father could always be found nearby, fishing at the shore's edge. He always wore his straw cowboy hat, an old short sleeve checkered shirt, and blue shorts.

Although I cannot remember seeing my dad ever catching a fish, I know that the moist ocean air and the gentle sound of distant crashing waves gave him a sense of relaxation and pleasure. He was in his element, staring past the horizon as if he was somewhere else, and that somewhere else was all that mattered. Looking back, I regret that I was too impatient to join him in that "somewhere else"; he was unsuccessful in his efforts to invite me into his world.

When I was a teenager the one place I was able to connect with my father was, not in the great outdoors, but in our own backyard – in a metal shed. The shed was big enough for only two people to sit in and was mostly filled with old tools and had a wooden workbench. On the walls were several family pictures. Although the shed was metal, it had the smell of the weathered oily wood stained work bench, greasy tools, and moist dirt floor. To anyone else this place was a typical backyard tool shed; to my father it was his sanctuary.

As a youth, I spent many memorable evenings in that shed watching my dad tinker and organize his prized ocean blue hiking backpack adorned with several patches displaying the many places they had been together. I remember admiring the patches from the Grand Canyon, Yosemite, the Sierra Nevada mountains, Mt. Whitney, and the Los Angeles Forest. Sometimes, I would catch my father looking them over as if each was a badge of honor.

Time and time again, he would meticulously organize his backpack, taking apart and reorganizing its contents: a sleeping bag or foam pad for sleeping, a flashlight, a small knife, food for three days, a two-man tent, a first-aid kit, and two water bottles. He did this while listening to his *Rancheras*, Mexican country music, on his old weathered radio connected between two extension cords from an electric socket in his bedroom. On occasion, he would set the radio station onto classical music, sounding more static than anything else because the antennae had being broken off years before.

After sorting through and organizing his belongings, he would then reverently hang the backpack back on the wall in its sacred place like a trophy representing his freedom and connection to nature. My dad enjoyed the idea that he had his backpack ready and prepared for any possible excursion, ready-to-go at a moment's notice.

As a kid, I treasured these moments with my father and was able to get to know him on a different level. Normally, I would only interact with him when he was exhausted from working or when I needed a source of discipline for my youthful and mischievous behavior. Watching him do something he enjoyed gave me a different idea of who my father was, and I liked what I saw.

As an older teenager I stopped being interested in such moments of closeness; I had other things on my mind. I became more focused on my part-time job, sports, and of course, the young women. I knew my dad wanted me to interact with him and to take part on his planned excursions, but I rejected almost all participation in outdoor activities with him.

This was not easily received. As the oldest son in a Mexican family, culturally, I was expected to be more involved with my father. But the reality was that I had become distant and uninterested in spending time with him. In addition to my new interests, I also could not help but feel resentment toward my parents who I felt were always too busy helping others to be interested in their own children.

Another factor was that my father did not drive. As a young man, he had been in a car accident that almost took my grandmother's life and vowed never to drive again. He never got behind the wheel and I missed the bonding experience many of my friends had driving with their fathers in cars.

I missed a lot of priceless opportunities...

Unlike me, my cousin Rey treated my father with respect and never missed an opportunity to stay close to him. Rey was thirteen years older than me and had lost his father at a young age. He saw my dad as a mentor. Rey was born and raised in East Los Angeles. He was intelligent, street smart, educated at the University of California, Los Angeles and was a veteran of the Vietnam War. His dad and my dad had been camping buddies and now Rey and my dad, the war veterans, shared a passion for nature and backpacking. Often, Rey would drive down from Los Angeles to San Diego and take my dad out on the trails.

I remember when they organized a hike to the summit of Mt. Whitney. My dad trained that entire year. He would walk three miles to work and three miles home. On the weekends, Rey and my dad took training excursions through the local mountains. When they were ready to hike Mt. Whitney, they took my older sister, Sonia and some of my cousins. My dad invited me several times to take part in that trip, but I declined. They all had a great time and I remember seeing pictures of the trip, feeling a little jealous.

Years later, my father took another excursion with my uncle Efrain, my younger brother, and more relatives. By that time, I had already graduated from high school and moved away to attend California State University at Long Beach. Like the miles between where I was and Mt. Whitney, I felt far away from backpacking.

One afternoon at the beginning of my fall semester, I was walking with my thoughts turned towards my father. Suddenly, I experienced intense stomach pain. Grabbing my stomach with my hands, I closed my eyes and attempted to catch my breath. I had a premonition, an intuitive understanding that something bad was going to happen to my father and that his time was limited. Once the stomach pain disappeared I immediately called my mother in San Diego from a campus pay phone to ask if my father was sick or in the hospital. She said in Spanish, "Your father is okay. He is camping in Yosemite with your brother and your uncle Efrain."

When my dad returned from his trip, he made an appointment to see his doctor. After several tests, the doctor told him that he had a serious case of esophagus cancer and only three months to live. Within those three months, my father went from being a strong, vibrant, active man, to one who was confined to his bed, thin and frail.

As a struggling college student with limited funds, visits to my parent's home in San Diego were reduced. "Are you coming home for the weekend?" my father asked me in a vulnerable tone.

Before I could answer, he had already given the phone to my mother, as if too worried I would say, "No."

"Yes, I will drive to the house on Friday afternoon. I should be home by dinner time," I told my mother. Her warm voice gave me comfort.

As I was drove south along the coast to San Diego from Long Beach the next day, I began thinking about the time I took my brown belt test in karate at the age of sixteen...

It was August 1976, a time when the martial arts were still new and exotic in non-Asian countries. I trained at two karate schools, one in National City and the other across the border on a dirt hill in Tijuana, Mexico where I took my brown belt test. The dirt road to the *dojo* was dangerously steep and narrow. This school was known for having several dynamic and courageous martial artists. I knew the experience was going to be daunting.

To pass the brown-belt test, I had to fight ten guys, one-on-one, during two-minute rounds at the Tijuana school. All ten fighters were rested, energized, and eager to have me earn my belt. Two guys before me, older and more experienced, did not pass their brown belt tests. During the fighting segment of the test, one had broken his arm and the other had dislocated his elbow. Even though I felt ready and had trained for this, I felt some anxiety before the exam.

During the sparring segment, I noticed my dad kept disappearing into the bathroom or going outside, not once or twice, but frequently. I did not understand why and jumped to the conclusion that he was disinterested in the major events of my life. I felt hurt he was not supporting me throughout this extremely demanding event.

I earned my brown belt that day. My face looked like a greasy cheese pizza from the constant punches and kicks I took. I could not eat or sleep normally for two weeks after that ordeal, but I was happy with my accomplishment. Not too many people in my environment were able to attain the Brown Belt level in karate at such a young age.

While I healed, I asked my mother why my father kept disappearing during the fighting segment of the exam. A part of me had already accepted the fact that my father was indifferent to anything important to me. To my surprise, my mother shared with me that my father was so nervous that he could not bear to see me go through the test; he was leaving the room to vomit.

This is the way my father expressed his concern for me... never directly expressing his emotional uncertainties but supportive in all my endeavors.

Thoughts of my father ran through my mind. I realized he was ill and sincerely wanted to see me again. I was not used to this side of him. My sisters had tried to warn me that he had been going through chemotherapy and had gone through drastic physical changes.

That Friday evening, when I entered my parent's house in National City, I tried my best not to reveal my feelings of shock. Instead of the domineering, robust head of the family, I saw a frail man with a cane. He had lost a lot of weight and was a ghost of himself. I found this experience unbearable and was not ready to acknowledge his condition or to fathom the thought of losing him. Instead, I tried to focus on the few opportunities I had left to recapture the lost relationship.

On another occasion, I entered his hospital room while he was peacefully resting with his eyes closed. As I put my hand on the metal railing of his bed closest to his chest, he reached out and covered my hand with his, thick and calloused; time stood still. I remembered how safe and protected I felt when he held my hand, a little boy, during long walks to the store or that time we went to Disneyland together, just the two of us. This rare moment lasted until three of my sisters suddenly barged noisily into the room and my father swiftly pulled his hand away, hiding his susceptibility from his daughters.

I jokingly said, "What's the matter, dad?" He looked at me realizing what he had just done; we normally dealt with uncomfortable moments with humor or sarcasm. I knew he did not want his daughters seeing his core emotions. This time, it was different. There were no sarcastic, catching remarks from him, only a glimpse of compassion in his eyes.

In December of 1985, in a small hospital room in National City, over thirty family members held a vigil as my father lay unconscious, struggling to breathe, tubes in his mouth and nose. I waited in the hospital lobby, making room for other family members. My niece Gabby innocently whispered, "Adios Tio" (good bye Uncle) five minutes before my father took his last breath. His physical body had ceased to do what we do so naturally.

My cousin Ricardo, from Mexico, tapped my shoulder to wake me up, to tell me that my father was gone; I already knew. At the moment he passed away I felt a warm cloud of air caress me and move up my chest and over my head.

During my father's funeral I counted over a hundred cars in the cemetery parking lot. While my father was not a rich man with material things, he was one who was wealthy with friendship and love. He was buried on a hillside next to the Pacific Ocean, a cemetery adjacent to the Cabrillo National Monument. I was only twenty-three.

The first three months without my father were difficult for all of us. It felt as if the heart of the family was gone and I just wanted to be left alone. Six months had passed before I could begin to come to grips with his loss.

My mother began to distribute his belongings. My brother got the embellished sword and knife he had taken from a German officer during the war. My sisters received photographs and some of his valuable camping equipment. Then my mother handed me my dad's blue backpack. I felt special; it was a connection to my father. I had a lot of great memories around that backpack. It was his pride and joy, and I felt honored. This motivated me to begin my own *journey to the mountain within my own soul.*

I began hiking by myself in places I knew I would not encounter crowds or noise. I liked spending weekends and vacation time on my own. I would occasionally go on a trip with a friend, but I preferred to be alone, far away from all the chatter of human company. My father's loss had created a deep emptiness in my soul that compelled me to find a way to reconnect with his spirit. With his blue backpack on my shoulders, I found myself walking his path, walking in his world.

The Journey Begins
My brother Carlos and two of my sisters, Yvette and Sonia, had spent a lot of time backpacking with my dad and knew a lot more than I did. Sonia worked as a Park Ranger, leading long excursions in Sequoia National Park. Yvette had been assigned to work at the Grand Canyon as a Supervising Law Enforcement Ranger. Both had managed to continue their relationships with my dad in their daily jobs outdoors. I wondered: *could I do the same, even*

though I had not connected with my father through backpacking when he was alive?

My brother Carlos and I made plans to hike the Grand Canyon during August, the hottest time of the year. My sister, Yvette, assigned to the Grand Canyon at the time, and her park ranger friends told us we were crazy to hike in 118 degree heat. But Carlos and I, set on hiking the Grand Canyon, paid them no mind and started our journey under the bright sun.

The day before we hiked to the bottom of the canyon and camped out, the next morning we began our trek upward on long canyon switchbacks. We grew exhausted from hiking in the scorching heat all day and stopped when the sun finally began to set. The canyon colors came alive with bright desert reds, soft shades of orange and purple detail. After spending most of the day on the trail, we were twenty minutes from the end of our hike and I was a half a mile ahead of my brother. The sweat from my forehead made its way into my eyes, causing me to squint as I sat down and rested on my backpack to wait for him.

Once I adjusted my eyes I could see in the distance, close to the trailhead of the canyon, the vision of a man who resembled my father and a woman who looked just like my mother. When my father was alive, my parents would often walk alone away from the drama of family, not saying much to each other, enjoying a quiet moment together. I looked out to the couple and tried to catch up with a renewed burst of energy, almost jogging. My energy could not keep up with my will to see them. I fixed my eyes on them as I stopped to catch my breath. I began walking again, but they disappeared.

I do not know what I had been seeing; it felt so real. Was I hallucinating because of the fatigue and the bright sun? They seemed so identical to my parents that I began to cry. I sat down on a big rock facing the panoramic view of the canyon, tears rolled down my dusty face. As my brother approached, he asked me what was wrong. At first, I could think of nothing to say. Then avoiding the question, I said that the sun had been in my eyes all day, and I was tired. That was the first time I had cried over the loss of my father.

Within that sadness I found beauty, and within that beauty, I found peace. I felt a shift inside that made me feel alive. After hiking the Grand Canyon with my brother, I experienced a transformation and was able to resolve the conflict in my soul. I experienced a form of healing the pain of losing my father; I was able to release the emotional baggage I had carried in my own invisible backpack.

After a few years of backpacking on my own and with friends, I realized that this was an experience that could help others resolve their issues and inner conflict. I decided it was time to share the experience with troubled teens that don't have the resources or know how to connect with the healing power of nature. That was how *Beyond Limits* started.

I always enjoyed sharing this story with the boys in the program… I wanted them to know that a greater man than me was the inspiration.

CHAPTER 4 FOCUS

Exploring our past can be very therapeutic. It forces us to look at past details our mind has ignored. This is important for all of us to find healing solutions. How can we ask our kids or clients to heal if we have not walked down that same path? The healing is enhanced when we are honest and acknowledge the negative and positive experiences from our own past. Walking through the healing process will make our lives fuller and more complete. We will become empowered healers.

CHAPTER V

BEYOND LIMITS PROGRAM

AFTER THE SUCCESS OF the first expedition, I continued to feel my father's guidance and spirit with me. After hiking one of the most demanding backpacking trails in the United States, I developed the skill of backpacking and felt the confidence of the experience. The following year I decided to coordinate another excursion.

This time, to alleviate recruitment setbacks, I decided to coordinate the *Beyond Limits Program* by creating a partnership with a school. The school would be a meeting place and provide additional resources that would allow me to work much closer with students and their parents. I called numerous schools in the Santa Ana Unified School District, being careful to promote my ideas in the most positive terms possible. Unfortunately, most of the schools were not ready to support an outdoor backpacking excursion in the High Sierras. I received polite rejections from almost all the schools, but one.

Just as I was about to give up on the idea of working with a local high school, I received a return phone call from Valley High in Santa Ana. The administrators were interested in meeting with me to discuss the possibility of a *Beyond Limits Program* on their campus. I met with the principal and academic counselor. The meeting was encouraging, and after much discussion we agreed to host the program at their school. My main liaison with the students and the school administration was Mr. Jones, the academic counselor. I was impressed with his dedication and compassion towards the students. He was grateful that *Beyond Limits* was going to assist the students who were having difficulties in school or were on the verge of expulsion.

We were provided with a classroom and met with students interested in taking the Mt. Whitney trek. I was able to share a slide presentation of our previous hiking excursions and answered any questions. The program started with forty eager participants. After the first orientation, the kids learned the fundamentals of mountaineering, team work, and intense physical conditioning. The group met twice a week. We needed as much conditioning as possible and began each session by running, we ran at the school track, at parks, and hiked in the local mountains.

Most of our sessions were based on physical training, but at times we stayed in the classroom and focused on Life Skills. I would invite guest speakers from the community to motivate the *Beyond Limits* participants. The students would listen to valuable perspectives from writers, musicians, law enforcement, and community organizers. The students showed appreciation for the guest speakers and what they had to say.

As time passed, it was a requirement for anyone who wanted to go on the second annual *Beyond Limits Mt. Whitney Challenge*: everyone had to be able to run five miles without stopping. After six months of training, there were nine strong, committed youth who were ready for the Mt. Whitney challenge. They had made it through the long haul.

Youth in the Program

The group of nine young men, mostly Latino males, committed to the program and actively participated in all the meetings. They truly proved they deserved their spot on the *Mt. Whitney Challenge Program*. Most of them were having problems in school; feeling pressured to join gangs, surrounded by poverty, and had family problems.

Among the participants was Oscar, recently released from Youth Guidance Center, an Orange County Juvenile Probation facility. Another student was Albert, who had trained on his own time for the trip while in custody. Then we had Jose, under a lot of pressure to join a gang. Pedro, was the youngest, but was determined to take part in the trip.

Many of these young men had rarely been out of their neighborhoods, much less in the mountains. They felt that the opportunity to hike through the High Sierras to the summit of Mt. Whitney was an honorable challenge for them. We had the opportunity to train these youth and properly prepare them mentally and physically. They were ready!

We scheduled the trip for July 1992. I wanted the youth to develop a sense of ownership toward the trip, and this meant I needed their participation. We had several carwashes, T-shirt sales, and a spaghetti dinner in the City of Santa Ana of which my mother was the head cook in the kitchen. The youth and volunteers set up the hall, served people, and cleaned up afterward. The young people learned that in order to reach a goal, one must work for it. The entire group raised most of the necessary funds to make the backpacking trip possible. Several adults volunteered and shared my vision for the second trip: Miguel Bernal and Octavio Gonzales from the previous trip, and Mario Fuentes, his brother-in-law.

Everything was falling into place except one critical element of the trip: four days before the excursion we were still short $300. Just when I had decided to use money from my own savings to pay the remaining balance for the trip, there was a knock on my door.

When I answered, I saw an older man with long, white hair placed in a loose ponytail. He looked rugged, and appeared to have an understanding of the hardships of life. As I opened the door, he asked in a direct manner, "Are you Luis Ruan?" I invited him in.

Sitting down, he said he had read the article in the local paper about the trip I was organizing to Mt. Whitney. "So how much money do you need?"

Humbly, I said, "Well, feel free to donate whatever you would like."

"I don't think you understood... I am asking how much money you need to make the trip a success."

"I need $300." I said in a quick breath.

"That's what I was asking," he said with a slight smile and wrote out a check for the needed amount. I thanked him and invited him for a meal or to visit a bit longer. He stood up, thanked me for working with the youth, wished me luck, shook my hand, and left. I never saw him again, but I remember him as a sort of an angel who removed the last obstacle to our excursion and answered my prayers.

The Campsite

I was much more relaxed this time around. I knew what to expect and was surrounded by seasoned adult backpackers and focused youth. We drove seven hours to Sequoia and arrived during the late afternoon. The group set up camp and organized the gear for the next day. Octavio and Miguel prepared a delicious pasta dinner; they were great cooks and enjoyed making creative dishes. The group was in high spirits and ready for the next day. We gathered all the youth and explained what they must do to complete the journey. I explained our expectations for the group:

1. We must work as a team.
2. Each must be responsible with their issued food.
3. All participants must be ready to be on the trail by 8 a.m.
4. We must respect each other.
5. No one was allowed to take anything that did not belong to them.
6. Everyone was responsible for their gear.
7. Absolutely no fighting.
8. Everyone had to work at keeping the environment peaceful.

After going over the expectations, we presented the itinerary of the nine-day trip. We went to sleep early that evening after preparing all our gear for our first backpacking experience.

On our first day of backpacking, we were dropped off at the Crescent Meadow Trailhead by 8:45 a.m. Once on the trail, the young men started with a swift hiking pace. I had to remind everyone to conserve their energy. We arrived at the Bearpaw campsite around 3 p.m., the group set up camp and went to bed early. The next day we were up early, ate a hardy breakfast and fumbled around trying to be ready on time. We hiked to Hamilton Lakes and had an extensive lunch period below a majestic waterfall. After lunch we hiked a few more miles to Hamilton Lake. We were instantly captivated by the beauty and decided to set up camp adjacent to scenic mountain lake. The guys took advantage of the lake and explored the area, fished, and went swimming.

After Hamilton Lake we made our way over to the Kaweah Gap at almost 11,000 feet then hiked down the mountain to the Big Arroyo Campsite. We set up camp and once we settled in, it rained, it hailed, and then it snowed. It was July and this unexpected weather forced us to spend an extra day. The young men spent the day resting, playing card games, and being typical teenagers. I could hear, and by the light of their flashlights, see the silhouetted figures of the boys laughing and enjoying themselves in their tents.

The next day before breakfast, we saw a bear near our campsite. When the bear saw our group it was startled and ran in the opposite direction. Five of the inexperienced youth foolishly decided to run after it as if it was a street dog, but the bear was much faster than these city kids. Fortunately, the frightened bear didn't stand its ground.

From Big Arroyo we hiked fifteen miles to Kern Hot Springs Campsite, the same location where Eddie and Peter almost fought with each other the previous year. This group of youth spent most of the evening in the hot springs and then transitioned to the cold water in the Kern River. They would sit in the hot springs for as long as they could, then walk a few feet and jump into the cold Kern River. They repeated this activity all night. At midnight, I could hear their voices, laughter, and could see the joyful shadows of the young men as they stood under the moonlight. I could not believe several of the youth were still enjoying the hot springs. I got up and told them to go to bed.

The next morning we hiked a mostly flat terrain of ten miles from the hot springs to Junction Meadow. It was a scenic hike that was adjacent to the Kern River. We could hear the constant echoes of the water flowing down stream and gurgling sounds of the water making contact with the rocks. The campsite was scenic and full of mosquitoes during the day.

We had four groups; each group had duties every day, from cooking, washing dishes, cleaning the campsite, to filtering drinking water. We organized duties in this manner to have the entire group function as a team. That evening it was my group's turn to cook.

I cooked tuna with macaroni and cheese. I cannot remember what I did differently, but, the macaroni was very sticky and chewy. Octavio and most of the youth had an amusing time making jokes about my cooking abilities. Octavio's humor soared at the opportunity. After the jokes, everyone ate from their emergency supply of food. The guys in my group politely asked me if they could help me cook next time. Pedro even recommended that upon returning home, I ask my wife to teach me how to cook.

First Group Challenge

From Junction Meadow, we began hiking the steep trails that are scenically beautiful, and the most physically challenging. We were hiking at an altitude of 10,000 feet on our way to the Crabtree Campsite when we came to a ledge overlooking a scary drop. It was here where the steep, narrow trail had been washed out by rain and replaced by a forceful waterfall. This was one of those moments of challenge and great fear that we had talked about as part of the High Sierra experience.

You can anticipate and count on experiencing at least one such moment, but you have no idea how it will present itself and how you will meet the obstacle while insuring everyone's safety. The adults quickly planned a strategy on how best to cross this forceful stream of water that was so close to a high cliff. We brought out the ropes and Miguel crossed to a safe area on the other side of the waterfall. Mario stayed behind to secure the ropes, while Octavio and I found a way to plant ourselves in the middle of the forceful waist-deep body of water to ensure no one slipped down the steep mountain.

We crossed the water one-at-a-time, forming a human chain that transported the backpacks and assisted the youth to the other side.

Everyone was helpful. Instead of complaints or worries or fearful comments, I heard sounds of laughter and joy in cooperation. The amazing part of this experience was that in working together, we developed a sense of trust in each other and became a team.

Young men need to develop trust in other men to affirm a positive sense of male camaraderie. Overcoming a physical obstacle reinforces a positive male interconnectedness. These opportunities, such as making it safely across dangerous waters as a group, instilled a cohesive sense of male solidarity, something rarely present in city life. For many of the young men in the group, the only male camaraderie they had witnessed was when it involved alcohol, drugs, violence, or gang activity.

After crossing the forceful stream below the waterfall, we had lunch nearby and fell asleep on the rocky, dirt trail. Exhausted, we were scattered all along the trail, and to any passersby, might have looked as if we had been victims of a natural disaster.

After an hour, we woke everyone up and made our way to the Crabtree Campsite Ranger Station by 4 p.m. The young men and Miguel set up camp, while Mario, Octavio and I went to talk to the ranger regarding weather conditions and to pick up our mail. We had mailed food packages to ourselves as a safety precaution, something backpackers can do to prevent running out of food. Ranger Rob glanced at us suspiciously with a look of distrust. We must have been an unusual sight from the usual backpackers he came across. He gave us everything we needed, and then seemed relieved when we went on our way to our campsite.

That evening everyone was in a joyous mood. Miguel had the youth singing an African song from South America. Miguel was able to play many instruments and had a captivating singing voice. We were all clapping and hitting our pots and pans in rhythm with the song, when Ranger Rob stopped by our campsite to check on us. He complimented the group and mentioned that he had a guitar available. Within minutes he returned with a steel string acoustic guitar. He started to sing some Axel Rose and Classic Rock songs and asked us to sing.

Miguel humbly took the guitar and sang some folkloric Latin American songs. All the youth knew the lyrics and sang along. Rob found the group to be entertaining and fun. He left our campsite close to midnight and invited us to his Park Ranger cabin for breakfast the next morning. We said our good nights to him and started to get ready for a restful sleep. I heard two of the youth still singing as they crawled into their tents.

The following morning we got our gear packed and walked a few minutes to the Ranger Station. We entered Ranger Rob's rustic one-bedroom cabin. He had cooked golden brown pancakes and served it up to us with fresh fruit and orange juice. Throughout the trip, our meals had consisted of powdered or dehydrated food, so eating pancakes with fresh fruit and drinking orange juice was a slice of heaven. Ranger Rob had bonded with all of us and was impressed with the commitment and energy of the group. After breakfast, we wished him well and hiked to the last campsite before Mt. Whitney, Guitar Lake.

We took our time hiking to Guitar Lake. The group arrived during the early afternoon. The team set up camp, took care of certain chores for dinner, and prepared for the following day. Once everything was complete, the youth were allowed to explore the area and to go fishing. Mario took three of the youth and caught golden trout. They came back to camp and cooked it for us with butter and Tapatio hot sauce.

The adults were able to relax and enjoy the sunset. We had dinner and went to sleep early. I wanted the group to get up at 4:00 a.m. and be on the trail in a half an hour. There were reasons for this: there was a lot of snow on the trail making it difficult to walk on, when the sun is out and the snow gets slippery. I did not want anyone in the group to slide down the mountain. The second reason was that lightning is common during the early afternoon. I wanted to avoid any possible opportunity of someone getting hurt.

We hiked in the darkness of the early morning. It was bone-chilling cold but as long as we stayed active, we stayed warm. The plan was to hike the summit as a group and walk close to each other as a precaution. After a few hours, the sun gave us the light we needed to see the Mt. Whitney summit. While I was excited to see the point of our final destination, I could also see a lot of snow on the trail, which was not an encouraging sign.

As we hiked onward, we arrived at part of the trail that was covered with snow. The snow was frozen solid because it had not been exposed to the sun, yet. Once the warmth of the sun made contact with the snow it would get slushy, slippery, and dangerous. I asked the youth to focus, to keep at least three feet behind the guy in front of them, and to communicate with the staff if anything happened. Once again, the staff regrouped and planned to distribute ourselves among the youth. I took the lead following a faint narrow snowy trail. Another adult stayed toward the back of the line and the rest were in the middle for anyone who needed help. The first stretch of the trail was a steep incline, one that was covered with snow and about a mile long.

At the halfway mark, I slipped and was about to tumble down the steep mountain. Fortunately, Oscar was behind me and quickly grabbed a hold of my right hand. With a strong grip on my hand and backpack, the young man held me until another adult was able to help lift me back up to the snowy trail. "Are you OK, Louie?"

Feeling helpless, yet secured, "I am OK! Thanks for your help." I was thankful for his quick reflexes and his strength, holding me suspended with my life in his hands. He pulled me up, dusted me off, and smiled proudly after I was standing on the trail again. I imagine he will always remember this as a moment of transformation and empowerment when he knew he had possibly saved a life.

After this scare, we cautiously continued to hike through the wet snow. The sun was rising and it was making the trail slushy. Fortunately by then, we had passed the areas covered in snow. About that time, the group approached the area where hikers can leave their backpacks and hike another two miles to the summit. As we were taking off our backpacks we saw Ranger Rob come out of nowhere. He had hiked cross country (off the main trail) to say goodbye to us. The youth were happy to see him. We invited him to hike up to the summit with us, but he was in a hurry to return to his job. Rob just wanted to say goodbye and wish us well. He then went down the mountain and disappeared.

Our team was successful hiking over Mt. Whitney. Unfortunately, we were not able to hike the two mile climb to the summit due to the threat of lightning. The group was a little disappointed, but they trusted the adults and understood that the safety of the entire group was of primary concern. We were able to take pictures and see the picturesque views that extended as far as Nevada.

The other side of the mountain

When it was time to make our descent, we began hiking again to the trail that led down to the other side of the mountain. We passed a group of fit middle-aged German hikers and asked them the condition of the trail going down the eastside of the mountain. They smiled and said "Ya goot, ya goot!" But I soon realized it was not going to be so "goot," when I noticed the part of the trail leading to the Whitney Portal was covered with snow.

It was approximately eleven miles down the mountain from the summit to the spot where we would meet our transportation home. The way down was covered with snow, and I could not see a safe trail down the mountain. I did, however, see a man-made chute extending down the mountain that slightly resembled an Olympic bobsled chute. I spoke with some of the adults, sharing with them that this terrifyingly steep path might be the only way down the mountain. We assessed the situation and agreed to go down one-at-a-time. One of the adults would go down as a test, and then if it worked, the youth would follow.

I agreed to take the test run, as I finished the conversation with the adults, I saw Pedro place himself in front of the chute. I asked Pedro to wait until I went first, with a mischievous expression he pushed off with his hands and began his journey down the steep mountain. I immediately trailed Pedro as we reached a safe flat area on the side of the mountain. From below I watched as each member of our group made their way down the mountain. At first, I could barely see the tiny black specks sliding down. But as they got closer, I could make out who was taking the slide. I saw some of the adults lock arms with the youth as they began their descent, breaking off from each other once they picked up speed.

Oscar, who had not yet smiled or laughed, who always concealed his face, day and night with dark sunglasses, was now smiling with a devious smile. As he walked by me, dusting off the snow from his pants, he said, "That is some fun shit... the best part of this trip, man!" He put his cool sunglasses back on and slowly strolled to the uncovered trailhead and proudly waited as if he was on a city street corner waiting for a ride.

We finished the hike down the mountain to Whitney Portal, and stopped at the trailhead of Mt. Whitney, to enjoy delicious hamburgers at my friend Doug Thompson's restaurant store. For many years, Doug and his family had always been very kind to us and supported the efforts we made with the youth. They all had incredible patience and understood the importance of the *Beyond Limits Program* and who it served.

Looking back, I think the first excursion to Mt. Whitney had been emotionally challenging because we did not know what to expect, and the behavior of the youth provided the greatest challenge. The second time, it was the weather that was the most difficult part of the trip. In both instances, all of us left with a better understanding of ourselves and of life. Every person involved in the *Beyond Limits Program* left stronger than before.

CHAPTER 5 FOCUS

When people are active in a worthy cause, the divine energy, spirit of the universe, is supportive of their quest. It is a journey that must be armed with unstoppable faith, conviction, and consistent action towards the desired outcome. This momentum attracts the right people and the right circumstances. People will always gravitate towards a noble cause. It is important to maintain a focused mentality to sustain the power of the vision, because grand ideas are often met with great adversity. The world needs more people who are willing to commit to a noble cause that will benefit humanity. *Be fearless in your quest.*

CHAPTER VI

OUTDOOR LEADERSHIP

IN AUGUST 1995, I TOOK the *Beyond Limits Program* in another direction. I felt the program was worth continuing. In keeping it alive, I chose to take new excursions with youth to keep the program fresh. I decided to take a new group to Mesa Verde, Colorado, where we would trek a different type of land.

Mesa Verde had some rugged terrain and I had prepped this new group of boys and girls to be ready. Most of the young people that participated in this trip hadn't participated in the previous excursion. We rented two twelve passenger vans and had a total of fifteen youth and five adults. Most of the youth came from Valley High, but a few I recruited were former incarcerated youth from the Orange County Probation Department.

The *Beyond Limits* staff had spent months working with them prior to the trip to establish a positive connection with all the youth. The former inmates and students worked well together. Everyone experienced a safe and enjoyable fourteen-hour drive to our destination.

Once we arrived on the Ute Reservation, we drove into the canyon to our campsite; two high jagged rock walls protected the dirt road. We drove slowly through the high canyon; the rock formations created the eerie appearance of countless ancient Native American faces imbedded in the long rocky walls. It was as if the old ones were watching us as we entered their land. I marveled at this phenomenon but said nothing; I looked at my youth and knew they witnessed the same thing. The canyon was several miles long and the rocks looked like the ancient ones acknowledged our arrival.

Our tour guide, Ernest House, was a Ute Native gentleman with whom I planned this trip. He was responsible for working with us while we were on Ute land. Ernest was a fit fifty year old Green Beret Vietnam Veteran, of medium height, wore a straw cowboy hat, and had a kind, peaceful demeanor. He enjoyed being with the youth and took us on daily hiking trips on the Mesa Verde to ancient ruins and other locations that most tourists would miss. I felt very fortunate to have him as a guide.

One day, Ernest took us on a ten-mile hike in an unfamiliar area of open, vast land, free of trail markers. I was using my compass, attempting to figure where we were situated when Ernest, walking with me, said, "Are you any good with that compass? If you had to, could you get everybody back to camp safely?"

I responded confidently, "Sure, no problem." Ernest said, "Really?"

"Yeah, if I had to, no problem..."

Ernest seemed to take this as a challenge. "Everyone, from this point forward, Mr. Louie gets you back. I will see you at camp."

He then ran off with his small backpack and his cowboy hat and disappeared. Everyone stopped dead in their tracks and one of the kids bluntly said:

"Can you really take us back?"

Another voice piped up, "Is Ernest coming back?"

And then another, more concerned, "Why did he leave?"

I told the group: "You guys need to relax. You panic too quickly. I know the way back to camp, besides I have a compass... let's start walking in *that* direction." But as we started hiking, I secretly felt a sense of panic. What if we never make it back? Will I be a bad leader?

After hiking for three hours, I found a shortcut that would save us three miles, but there was a thirty foot cliff that required rock-climbing.

I asked everyone to get into a circle and asked them if they willing to climb down this cliff or hike three more miles to the campsite. With a tired look on their faces, they agreed to climb down the cliff. Two agile young men, Pedro, from the second Mt. Whitney trip, and his buddy Joel, a cross-country running champion, agreed to hike down to test the level of difficulty. I then saw them skillfully climbed down the cliff like two cats negotiating themselves down a tree. The first to make it down yelled out, "It is a piece of cake, Louie!"

After they gave me the word, I proceeded to go down and asked the adults if they could make sure the youth climbed down one at a time. I placed myself halfway down the climb to make sure people did not panic. I made continuous jokes to help the youth relax, the kids with a sense of humor eagerly joined in.

Eventually, we were able to relax and to finish our descent free of injury. Once the challenge was completed, we hiked a few miles to our campsite and prepared for dinner.

After a gratifying meal, I asked everyone to express how the experience affected them. One young man calmly stared at the youth and then directly looked at me, said: "I was scared when we were rock climbing. If Louie would have panicked and lost it, we all would have lost it!" The majority of the youth nodded their heads in agreement. We found out later that Ernest had been praying for us, leaving tobacco offerings near us as we climbed down the cliff.

That night before sleeping, I thought about what that young man had said. I was well aware of my responsibility to keep the youth and adults safe, but I never gave much thought to the emotions I projected. I learned from this excursion that if a leader projects fear in potentially dangerous situations, the group will react to that fear with a lack of confidence and perhaps make the potential for real danger. When a leader projects sincere confidence and awareness, it will give the participants the confidence they need to keep themselves safe.

After the circle with the youth, Ernest shared with me that he was not far away; he was able to see everything. Ernest wanted everyone to work as a team and to learn from the experience. He had bonded with us, staying to share our meal, taking us further on a sacred trail of the Anasazi people, and sharing his wisdom and prayers. On our last day we repelled off of a two-story cliff, an exercise of trust and focus. He closed the day with a talking circle where the youth were able to express their thoughts and emotions. There were stories of triumph and tears of joy.

Seven Basic Principles of Outdoor Leadership

1) *Youth at-risk need to be kept busy with productive activities*

My dad inadvertently followed this principle of keeping active kids occupied. My relatives used to call my dad "the sergeant" for the work assignments he gave people who claimed to be bored. He was a bit bossy, but he had a way of reaching the troublemakers of the neighborhood. It was common to see a kid who had broken a window the night before, pulling weeds in my front yard with a focused look on his face. These kids seemed to enjoy working in some peculiar way. Perhaps it made them feel needed, but, in any case, it was something constructive to do that produced tangible results. I learned from my father the importance and usefulness of keeping youth occupied and focused on productive tasks.

2) *Young people need a physical reference point of success*

Hiking the second higHiking the second highest mountain in the United States, or hiking to the deepest section of the Grand Canyon in one day are notable achievements and healthy examples of what can happen when a youth is prepared, guided by mentors and is given the opportunity to excel. Accomplishments will be stored in the psyche of an individual crystallizing a strong belief in the abilities of that individual to reach his or her highest potential, as a youth and as an adult.

3) *Young people need to see healthy examples of success in their environment*

Too often, young people only have negative examples in their lives instead of positive role models. When I worked in East Los Angeles, I remember meeting Lamont Hyde, a man who worked in the music industry. He carried himself with a confident flair and an approachable demeanor. He had a recording studio that was used by most major hip-hop artists, and he did looping for major Hollywood movies. When I visited Lamont's office/studio I was impressed by all that he was able to accomplish. What impressed me the most was that he was a mentor to one of the young men who lived in the Pico-Aliso Projects in Boyle Heights, East Los Angeles.

When I asked him how he became so successful, Lamont shared with me that he had a difficult past living in South Central Los Angeles. As a child, he had a neighbor across the street that consistently woke up early and went to work in the recording industry. After work, he spent hours rolling up long cables and organizing them for the next day. Lamont shared that he never talked to this man, but the image of this hard-working neighbor left a profound impact on him. Lamont wanted to follow his neighbor's example, working hard and excelling at entry-level jobs in the recording industry up until his present success.

If positive role models are not made real to our youth, they will assume they do not exist. I remember an internship I did with the Santa Ana Probation Department, in which I was assigned to several Chicano field probation officers. The interaction I had with them made my dream of working in the probation department real and approachable, these probation officers had similar struggles compared to my own. With this role model connection, I was able to connect to my goal. It is the same with youth. They need positive examples to mirror.

4) *Taking youth outside of their limited environments will open their minds*

Sadly, most of the youth who participated in *Beyond Limits* had rarely traveled outside of their *barrios* or neighborhoods. When they experienced different environments and people from different cultures, they were able to reflect on who they were and where they fit, culturally. Because of this experience, many youth who took part in the *Beyond Limits* excursions were interested in learning more about their culture.

One young woman, after an excursion to Navajo Land, took the initiative to attend a university in Michoacán, Mexico. There, she experienced a new cultural depth and enhanced her Spanish language skills. This young woman eventually completed school and later became a high school teacher.

5) *Reinforce the importance of understanding cultural dynamics*

Cultural knowledge, often devalued in the education system and in the media, is instrumental in developing a healthy self-esteem. It is imperative to have authentic cultural education which we accomplished by providing lessons on Andean music and Latin American guitar and by traveling to Native American reservations across the United States. These experiences sparked interest in cultural identity, provoked reflection, and with reflection, action.

6) *People honor that which they work for*

The level of appreciation is deeper when the group works as a team to reach specific goals. In our first excursion to Mt. Whitney, the more we did for the youth, the less respect and appreciation we received. After that trip, I made a commitment to recruit potential students from the very beginning to work together for a common goal.

The excursion that followed thus became everyone's trip, not just a trip that my friends and I financed. It was much more effective to work together and to draw from the support of the community through car washes, spaghetti dinners, T-shirt sales, and concerts. It was also an example of what can be accomplished by working as a team. If the trip was funded and given to the youth, they would not have known how to appreciate it.

7) *Create a Healing Space*

During my *Beyond Limits* year, I knew several people who were more than happy to run Native American sweat lodges and healing circles for the youth. These individuals did this because they knew young people need a vehicle to vent, let go of anger and resentments. We did not force the youth to take part in them, but most participated. The young people were given a chance to listen to the problems of older men and women, to express their own issues as well as receive positive guidance from others who had had similar life experiences.

CHAPTER 6 FOCUS

As a leader you are a walking breathing example of how to interact with the world. Participants are watching and studying every move you make. If a leader projects a sincere confident demeanor, it will provide the group the assurance they need to be safe and to fulfill their goals. You must be the epitome of what you are attempting to instill. A leader is always well prepared and willing to go much further for the purpose of encouraging those in their circle. He/she is the first one to wake up and the last one to go to sleep. A well-rounded leader has the ability to plan an activity or excursion in specific detail. They will know how to motivate and inspire people to do their best, in their example and conviction. A leader yields public recognition to those that have worked diligently.

CHAPTER VII

NAVAJO LAND

IN THE SUMMERTIME OF 1995, on my way home from the Ute
Reservation in Southern Colorado, I pulled into a gas station near
Page, Arizona off Highway 160. I needed a break from driving a
van full of eight energetic teenagers. They had been asking for an
opportunity to buy souvenirs, so I gave them twenty-five minutes to
complete their shopping. I was somewhere near the border of the
Navajo Nation.

I parked the van, in front of an old family run market adjacent
to the gas station, a social area for the local residents. I staggered
out of the van and walked into the store. I bought us some snacks,
placed the food in the van, and strolled to the front of the store to
sit in the shade while the youth shopped.

As I sat on down on a bench next to the door, I could see the
local people getting gas and shopping at the market. Most were
Native Americans and a few tourists. I noticed an elderly Navajo
couple leisurely walking into the market. The man was thin and lean
wearing weathered cowboy boots and a cowboy hat that made
him appear taller than he was. His wife wore colorful clothing, a

traditional blue velvet dress and carried herself in a regal manner. Something about them caught my attention. They strolled slowly, as elderly people usually do, with a sense of dignity.

Fifteen minutes later, I stood up and opened the weathered wooden screen door to help them out. Each acknowledged me with a warm smile as they walked out of the market, then watched them quietly walk back to their old white Ford truck. I could feel they were compassionate people who probably had many grandchildren. I thought about how beautiful they moved in rhythm with each other and how they both fit in with the scenic desert landscape.

Within a few minutes, their vehicle disappeared into the horizon toward Navajo Land. At that moment, an intuition hovered over me and a silent conscious decision came out of nowhere: I knew I was going to work on the Navajo Nation... I could see it and feel it. The Navajo Nation had always held an appeal for me. I admired how the Diné (Navajo people) were able to practice their culture without the poisons of the dominant society. It reminded me of the Huichole Indians in Central Mexico who dress in their traditional attire in the big cities, regardless of mainstream Mexican ridicule. I admired their poise, dignity, and respect for their culture.

Several weeks passed and my silent decision to work on the Navajo Nation was forgotten. Upon returning home, I was more concerned about my job, paying bills, and preparing for next summer's *Beyond Limits* excursion.

Months later, I called the Navajo Tourist Department to inquire if there was someone in Navajo Land willing to talk to the youth from Beyond Limits about their culture. I explained how I was planning another backpacking trip to Colorado the following summer. I was looking for someone to educate the youth on Navajo culture with a lecture or slideshow presentation. My plan was to stop there for a short period of time on our way to Colorado. The following day a pleasant Navajo woman returned my call. She gave me the phone number of several resources; one contact was the Chinle School District Curriculum Center.

I made contact with the Chinle Curriculum Center staff and they were very interested in creating collaboration. They expressed concern about their youth and were open to innovative ideas and approaches to redirecting teen violence. After many conversations with representatives, we discussed and planned a week-long union between the youth from California and the youth from Navajo Land in Arizona. I was amazed at how the organizing and planning of this gathering was met with such enthusiasm. The *Beyond Limits* team had invested many hours to make it happen and the Chinle School District staff did an amazing job getting everything ready for our visit. I recognized that everything had fallen into place the way it was supposed to be, and my initial intuition had prepared and motivated me to take part in this event. The gathering was assisted by a power greater than all of the organizers.

We spent six months organizing every aspect of the encounter making sure that the youth would have the best experience possible. We wanted to make this trip a healthy exchange for all the youth. Our main goal was to create an environment which facilitated positive dialogues regarding two important points: youth violence and the importance of cultural awareness.

First Cultural Encounter

In April of 1996, twenty-one youth and nine adults from the Beyond Limits Program began their excursion to Navajo Land. We made a weekend detour to Zion National Park, Utah. From there we drove six hours to Chinle, Arizona in the central area of the Navajo Nation. We arrived in Chinle around mid-afternoon on a Sunday. Patches of snow could be seen on the side of the road. When I stepped out of the van I felt the shock of the thick cold wind.

I immediately called Marjorie Thomas, an elder who had volunteered to have us stay on her land. She asked us to call her, Grandma Thomas. She was a retired educator, former school administrator, and a school board member for the Chinle School District. She told me she would meet us at a Bashas' grocery store parking lot.

When she arrived, Grandma Thomas wore glasses, a traditional hair bun, and a long skirt with a warm jacket. We greeted one another and then followed her home. She had an impressionable commitment to her people, especially the youth. Grandma Thomas and her son Leon Sky Horse and family lived just outside of Chinle. They had a home on several acres of land with sheep sprinkled on the immense landscape. We camped out in our tents, about 200 feet from their home.

Open Space

The land was breathtaking. It was heavy-jacket weather at night and colder in the morning. The bitter wind brushed against us like a wet blanket; the air was thick. Regardless of the weather, whenever I had a moment to myself I would marvel at the terrain. The land was covered with layered orange, reddish- brown dirt. I could see the blue-grey sage brush scattered on the hillsides with evergreen, and some cottonwood trees. The combination of the fresh damp dirt, juniper trees, and sage brush, created an unforgettable sweet aroma. The dirt roads seemed endless with scattered isolated homes in the distance; the land disappeared into the horizon. The setting gave me the urge to just jump out of the van and run endlessly. The thought of running free on this welcoming landscape lifted my heart. It was a well-deserved joy not to be forced to listen to loud music, police helicopters, or be trapped in the busy energy of city traffic.

Most of us were not accustomed to see the land so free, the earth so untouched, the world so alive. In the city, all of our natural empty spaces are manipulated for business and for profit. Land in the city is perceived as a dollar value or utilized to satisfy the demands of overpopulation. Society continues to take the land in the name of progress. It saddens me to see the natural land areas that were once open when I was a child, now filled with mini-malls, model homes, and franchised businesses that take the uniqueness away from the community.

Navajo Land is approximately 27,000 square miles and I saw how free the earth can be. I marveled at the overwhelming beauty it carried. The area includes Arizona, parts of Utah, Colorado as well as New Mexico. It is considered the biggest land mass of Native land in the United States.

Every night, we enjoyed a warm colorful campfire. With crackling sounds of the fire, Grandma Thomas and her son Leon sang Navajo songs and Leon would then end the night by telling us a traditional story. Leon sang with a polished high-pitched voice and was knowledgeable about his culture. The songs and stories added a nice closing to the day's events. The young people were attentive during Leon's talks. It put a smile on my face to see the young people having fun doing something so simple.

Importance of Group Meetings

Along with a full day of activities, we also had nightly circles. These consisted of groups discussing issues that surfaced throughout the day, positive events, and conversations about the plans for the next day. Sometimes, personal issues would arise with the youth that needed ironing out, or adult issues that needed immediate attention. Putting out these types of small fires kept situations from escalating. If a youth was having behavioral problems, it had to be addressed as soon as possible. If not, the situation would more than likely get worse. I learned it is better to deal with group problems immediately, and like a fire that is left alone, problems might grow and become more volatile. With these youth, I kept to my rule of resolving issues within a 24-hour period, or sooner.

Now of course, it is human nature to test each other's limits until mutual respect is established. With the youth, we dealt with issues either privately or in an open circle where people were allowed to voice their concerns. I learned that by taking people away from their normal environment, issues would naturally surface, especially if members of the group do not make an effort to adapt to one another. We had our share of dramatic incidents. It was beneficial because it forced them to face and to acknowledge their negative behavior. It was important for the teenagers and sometimes the adults to look at their behavior because that acknowledgement assisted the group in obtaining a level of harmony, and creating harmony takes effort. The group meetings taught me about the importance of healthy communication.

Cultural Education

For most of the kids and staff it was their first time on a Native American Reservation. One particular youth thought he was going to see Native people living in tepees and hunting with bow and arrows. Later, after observing the similarity between Mexicans and Native Americans, he said to me, "They look like us."

Another young man approached a young Native American woman at a roadside jewelry stand on the way to Chinle and attempted to communicate with her in Spanish. She was selling necklaces and he asked in Spanish for the price of a traditional necklace he liked for his mother and was surprised when she didn't understand. The young woman responded with a friendly giggle toward the confused young man.

He walked away from the jewelry stand, and approached me slightly upset. "Hey Louie... Why don't they speak our language? Are they embarrassed to be Mexican or what?" As he lifted his hands in frustration, I tried not to laugh at his naiveté, and explained to everyone that those folks were not Mexicans.

"They call themselves Diné, and they have their own language and culture... They have a traditional Native American way of life that has been maintained through many historical hardships. They are dark like us because we also possess that ancient Native connection."

I remember thinking how such experiences were educational for both the youth and the adults, and I was honored to have been a part of this unique experience.

Positive Peer Pressure

The majority of the kids we took were Latino. Many of these young people lived in communities surrounded by gang violence, drug/alcohol abuse, lacked job opportunities, and attended overcrowded schools in impoverished neighborhoods. A few of the participants were active gang members.

The way we normally were able to get the kids to connect to one another was through positive peer-pressure. I found time and time again, these kids would often listen more intently to one of their peers than an adult authority figure. We used this understanding to our advantage whenever we could.

On the first day in Chinle, during a lunch gathering at the high school, I overheard a conversation between the youth. A male Native American teenager was talking to Angel, who happened to be an active gang member.

"Hey, what is it like in the city?" he asked. "Are there a lot of gangs where you come from? What are the gangs like? Is it easy to join a gang?"

The handful of youth that were standing around instantaneously turned their heads towards Angel and ceased their conversations.

Angel was only sixteen. He stood up to answer the question. He was a gang member from the city of Santa Ana. Angel was a born leader; the type of kid who could do a lot of good, or could inflict an enormous amount of damage with his natural charisma.

"Why do you want to know about that stuff?" he asked. "Look what you guys have here. You have a lot of land and clean air and you still value your history and have all your ceremonies. We don't have anything like that where I am from...You guys are lucky! We have to deal with a lot of people in the city, overcrowded schools and aggressive cops. We live in a concrete jungle!" He finished his words with the perfect amount of emotion and conviction.

I saw those young Native Americans react with stunned expressions on their faces. Perhaps they were expecting a different response from the young man from California. And what I enjoyed about that situation was that it was spontaneous. The youth who were there had listened to Angel. His words had penetrated their hearts and minds. Angel's communication did a lot to discourage gang violence in that one moment. I stood there with my back to them, pretending to be busy and invisible, smiling inside.

Cultural Activities

On day two, we participated in a traditional Native American sweat lodge. The school district had provided buses to transport students and adults to the locations. In Diné society, the men and woman sweat with their own gender. We had three sweat lodge locations for the men and one for the women. One group went into the Diné traditional sweats that are made of the earth. They resemble a small dwelling made of dirt that is caked on a cone-like structure. The inside is lightly dug into the dirt, around five feet in diameter. Two other groups went into the Plains Indian sweat lodges made with circular willow frames, covered in blankets.

Even though the structures are different in construction, the ceremony is similar in purpose and design. The sweat lodge ceremony is for healing of the physical, emotional, mental, and spiritual parts of us. It helps the participant get back into balance and in harmony with their environment.

Before going into the sweat, the sweat lodge leader and his helpers cook volcanic rocks the size of large melons on a large fire pit for about three hours until they are lava-red. When the rocks are ready they are placed on the north section of the sweat lodge (Diné) or in the middle (Plains), and then everyone enters the sweat lodge clockwise. An authorized individual or medicine person facilitates the ceremony.

While participating in a sweat lodge, everyone should see this time as one of prayer, meditation, and expression. Packed like sardines inside the sweat, through the darkness you can hear the hissing of water poured onto the glowing red rocks and the beautiful songs sung by the sweat leader. We heard prayers in the Diné language; we heard the rumbling of everyone praying concurrently. There was the smell of damp earth and burned cedar leaves and sage brush. This is how we made our connection to the Great Spirit.

In the sweat lodge, several youth from *Beyond Limits* shared some of the hardships and trails they were facing back home. After their testimony, the sweat leader expressed words of encouragement for the youth and recited beautiful poetic prayers in his language. After several hours of prayer in the sweat, we crawled out with a purified mind and spirit, a rebirth.

Reborn and Purified

The sweat lodge was a new and positive experience for the youth. Our group did well, meaning they were able to learn and endure the heat, emerging relaxed and in high spirits. The *Beyond Limits* youth and some of the Diné youth from Chinle High School spent most of the morning and afternoon in the sweat lodge. We were exhausted after the ceremony was complete. Later we cooked dinner, sang songs with Leon and went to bed.

On day three, we were invited to participate in a cultural presentation/ceremony at Diné Community College in the town of

Tsaile, Arizona. The college had a large Hogan, a traditional circular structure (hexagonal or octagonal in shape), a dwelling space used for traditional ceremonies. The door to a Hogan always faces east with the medicine people sitting on the west facing the door. Like a sweat lodge, one must walk into a Hogan clockwise. There were over sixty people participating in the event; including, the district superintendent, curriculum center staff, teachers, maintenance workers, students, and the *Beyond Limits* members.

The purpose of the ceremony was to help the *Beyond Limits* youth better understand the Diné culture. For more than an hour, a professor from the college shared eloquent teachings about the Diné. His lecture was profound and comprehensive, describing the complexity of their worldview, teaching us that there is richness to Diné philosophy. As we all sat patiently on the earth, the professor asked that we pray together.

His helpers then passed out a squarely cut cornhusk to each of us along with a single tobacco pouch. We placed the tobacco in the husk and rolled it tightly. As we began smoking, the medicine man instructed everyone to bless themselves with the smoke and to pray. I noticed that all the Diné folks were in a focused meditative state of praying and sending their prayers with the smoke to the divine. As everyone was praying in unison, a school district maintenance man was moved to sing a traditional spiritual song in resonating hypnotic voice. The focused praying, the traditional song, and the strands of tobacco smoke gently rising, created a sacred and unique moment that was shared collectively. It was so natural for them to make that connection. Several of the *Beyond Limits* youth prayed, while others were slightly distracted attentively observing what everyone else was doing. Overall, it was a distinct experience to be part of a collective prayer.

Prior to the ceremony, I explained to the youth how the tobacco was a vehicle for prayer and communication with the Creator. Mainstream society views tobacco as an unhealthy addiction, while Native people throughout the Americas have always used it in a sacred manner: to connect with the divine.

During the following days, we had talks at the high schools, junior highs, elementary schools, and community centers. We had to split up the *Beyond Limits* youth because they were in such high demand. Besides the interactions in classroom settings, we were treated to a hay ride through the beautiful Canyon De Chelley. This canyon is spectacular. It has high-colored sandstone walls and cliffs. Some of the cliffs have ancient Anasazi (ah-nuh-SAH-zee) dwellings. These dwellings have been in existence since about 1200 BC to 1300 AD, the ancestors of the present day Pueblo, Zuni, and Hopi Native American nations.

On day four, we rented twenty horses for the youth and several of the local teens brought their own. The city youth were eager to learn how to ride a horse and had to do so, quickly. It was entertaining to see these fearless city kids learning the basics of horsemanship. Watching the youth was more entertaining than a comical movie. I saw one of my boys get bucked a few feet in the air and land on the soft canyon sand, landing with a big smile on his face. He stood up laughing and dusted himself off. Everyone laughed along with him. Another kid could not get his horse to move, while another could not get his horse to stop. Looking back,

I think maybe the horses were having the most fun. Fortunately, the local students were patiently assisting the *Beyond Limits* youth.

Later, we had a delicious cookout in the Canyon. We were entertained by a renowned Powwow champion, traditional grass dancer, Jonathan Windy Boy from Rocky Boy, Montana. He shared entertaining stories and had the young people join him in singing Native songs. They enjoyed the stories and songs.

The canyon was a pivotal experience. It was nice to see the youth, adults, teachers, administrators, and parents, enjoying an afternoon of fun interaction. With satisfied stomachs and full hearts, we returned to our campsite by the late afternoon.

Powwow

On day five, we participated in a Powwow at the Chinle High School basketball gym. A modern Powwow is an event where Native people gather to honor Native culture. It is also where old friends reunite, new friends are made, and lots of socializing takes place along with Native singing and dancing. There is generally a dancing competition with prize money. People are honored for their deeds.

During the Powwow that evening, I was deeply moved when the community honored our group with a traditional song; the host drum sang a song of honoring. Next they asked the *Beyond Limits Program* to line up in the middle of the gym. As we stood it seemed like the entire Chinle community approached us to give each of us a sincere handshake. It was inspiring to see the *Beyond*

Limits youth happy and respected, many of them having never experienced being publically acknowledged and honored in that way. That evening, before leaving the Powwow, my friend Jerome Towne, a youth counselor at the Chinle Treatment Center, invited us to a sweat lodge ceremony for early that next morning.

On day six, we attended our last sweat. It was powerful and insightful for the youth. The ceremony lasted two hours. Afterwards, we met up with the others at the school parking area and reluctantly started driving back toward California. During the evening we stopped at a rest stop to eat and sleep. There we camped out near the picnic benches and slept in any area that was available. The next day in the afternoon we arrived back to Santa Ana, tired and with a renewed outlook.

In the years to follow, the *Beyond Limits Program* participated in three more youth and community exchanges with the Chinle School District. That last exchange, organized by the Chinle Curriculum Center, had 500 youth participate from across Navajo Land. The following year, *Beyond Limits Program* organized a conference at University of California at Irvine and the Chancellor allowed us to use three large meeting rooms for the conference. We organized a conference tailored for Navajo educators and community agencies. A total of 100 people participated with some of the top speakers and educators in the area addressing issues relating to youth at-risk behavior.

CHAPTER 7 FOCUS

Taking inner city youth outside of a comfortable environment to experience a distinct culture, forces them to reflect on their culture and place in the world. This type of reflection gives birth to a healthy self-esteem. It motivates young people to look deeper into who they are and what they will become. Cultural identity is crucial in the development of a teenager. Many young people of color become oblivious to the importance of cultural knowledge. Youth are often bombarded with inaccurate negative cultural information feeding into a disempowering self-concept. Cultural awareness creates healthy and balanced adults.

CHAPTER VIII

WORKING IN
INDIAN COUNTRY

AFTER THESE CONFERENCES AND cultural exchanges, I was invited to participate as a gang awareness/youth at-risk consultant in many of the communities on Navajo Land. Ten years in the probation department taught me about human behavior and high-risk youth. I felt confident in sharing my experiences. Public speaking soon developed into a full-time job. Most of my consultant work was in different communities across the United States and in Canada. The topics I spoke on were on gang awareness, youth violence and community leadership. I loved traveling into different communities and learning about the differences and strengths of each tribe.

Most of my work was on Navajo Land. During that time gang violence was in its early stages in the Navajo Nation, and not nearly at the level I experienced in Southern California. However, some of the communities I came across were well on their way to experiencing the negative ramifications of gang violence. I was sent all over Navajo Land and gave presentations in many of their rural communities. On one of the consultant trips as I was about to go home, a friend that worked for the tribal government invited me to speak at the Navajo Council Chambers in Window Rock for an assessment of their youth violence situation.

In their form of government, to be invited to speak at the Council Chambers is like speaking in front of the House of Representatives or the U.S. Senate. Each town on Navajo Land has a Chapter House where town meetings are held and where political decisions are made. Each one has a representative that takes part in decisions on behalf of the area they represent and attend gatherings at the Council Chambers to vote on major decisions for the Navajo Nation.

I felt honored. I waited in a small room for my turn to speak. As the First Lady Regina Hale formally introduced me, I nervously approached the podium. I looked up towards the audience and saw a large room full of Dine'/Navajo Leaders. They sat there patiently and attentively as I began my talk. I explained that culturally, they already had all of the tools to deal with the problem of gang violence, "What I have seen in California is extreme, but you can turn it around with hard work and more programs that deal with youth issues."

I shared with them that gang violence is a symptom of other unresolved societal issues such as poverty, cultural breakdown, lack of employment, domestic violence, drug/alcohol abuse, and teen suicide..."Young people are asking for our help with their behavior."

Following my assessment presentation, the leaders were appreciative of my input and gave me a warm applause. In the years that followed, I continued doing my workshops and returned many times. I was seen so often on Navajo Land that they thought I lived there and was treated as a local.

Traveling with Gang Members

On one trip, I took three youth with me to conduct a series of workshops. These boys were actively involved in gang violence. Two of them were considered *hard core* by law enforcement and probation. I was up for the experience.

Joseph was the oldest, seventeen, lean, tall, and wore baggy clothes and had a shaved head. I met him while he was in a probation facility. He seemed more relaxed then, when he was in custody. Outside of the facility, he was withdrawn and had a gloomy disposition.

Marcos was sixteen, stout with native features and a shaved head. I met him while he was at the same probation facility. His father had died when he was young. He had witnessed a lot of violence in his young age and had been a bystander during a murder prior to his incarceration.

Then there was Jose who had been actively involved in *Beyond Limits*. He had many close calls with gang membership. During one incident, an attempt was made on his life for trivial reasons. Gang members chased him and fired several shots. He had been pressured to join a gang and decided to get involved with the *Beyond Limits* program instead, to get away from his troubles.

I observed that these gang members were different, now that they were released from custody. While incarcerated they seemed rested, well-fed, and healthy. On the outside, they looked tired, stressed, and high strung; on survival mode. They seemed like different people and I didn't know what to expect from them.

In order to create healing, we must first understand the problem.

During these workshops, the talks were about gang violence and community mobilization. The three youth were there to share their stories and help create understanding and hope for the folks on the reservation. After three days of workshops, we accepted an invitation from a traditional healer from the community to participate in a sweat lodge ceremony near the foothill of the Chuska Mountains.

Once we arrived at the ceremony, I could tell it was going to be a packed house, meaning we would be sitting like sardines in a small area with unrelenting heat. I saw a lot of people who seemed eager go into the sweat.

This sweat lodge was more of a plains-style sweat with willow branches forming a circular dwelling. It was covered with army canvases and blankets to prevent light from entering. Red-hot rocks were placed in the middle of the sweat four times. Water gently spilled on the rocks created intense heat and steam. The sweat lodge ceremony is traditionally four rounds consisting of fifteen minutes each, or more, usually much more. After each round we would come out and get some air and recover. When everyone was ready, we would go back in. The first round was almost an hour long and extremely hot for us city folks.

After the first round the young men who were with me said in a decisive manner, "That's it! Louie, these old farts are going to make *Carne Asada* out of us... We ain't going back in, man. These guys are nuts!"

I tried to encourage them to be strong and to finish the sweat lodge ceremony. I guess I was not very convincing. They were done. In a way, I could not blame them in that it was extremely hot. I continued the ceremony without them. It was a strenuous sweat and I had a hard time staying in there myself, but didn't want to offend the men who were being hospitable to us.

Since these young men had a lot of anger and drugs in their system, it made it more difficult for them to endure the heat. Negative lifestyles, anger, drugs, alcohol, and trauma make it difficult to sit still in a sacred ceremony. Troubled people have an internal battle: being healed and resolving their trauma. Once the negativity is released, the mind and body are able to balance.

What was interesting was how these young men saw themselves as *tough guys*. In some aspects they *were* tough in that they lived harsh lives. But the strength that they lacked was spiritual strength, mental focus, emotional balance, and physical endurance. The old men in the sweat lodge got a kick out of the young men.

One of the medicine men jokingly said, "Hey Louie, I thought those guys were tough, tell them to get back in here!" Then a roar of laughter came from the older medicine men inside the sweat lodge.

When the ceremony was complete I crawled out of the sweat lodge dizzy, nauseous, and relieved to breathe fresh air. I lay down on a rug until my rapid heartbeat calmed down. I looked up at the sky with a refreshed new outlook. Underneath the faint light of the moon, steam rose from my sweaty body as I gazed out at the evening stars glittering like bright Christmas lights. Once my body adjusted, I felt as if I had left all of my worries in the ceremony; I felt euphoric; a positive shift had occurred.

That night we drove back to our rooms at the college and had a restful sleep from an active and spiritually cleansing day. The next day we were scheduled to speak to a few more communities before returning to Southern California. We were exhausted from the many presentations we took part in across the Navajo Nation. I drove the young men home on a Saturday morning. They slept most of the way, waking up only to eat and to gaze pensively out the window at the boundless desert landscape. Later that evening, exhausted, we arrived in Santa Ana. I dropped off all the youth before finally going home.

I kept in touch with the participants through their probation officers. Joseph ended up doing some hard time in state prison. Marcos served two years in prison and then managed not to return. Jose works in upper management, bought a house in the suburbs, got married and has two healthy sons.

Healing takes time and the individual's willingness to do the work are key factors.

Important Teaching

I recall a time during my first public speaking sessions when I was invited to conduct a training in an isolated area in the northwest section of New Mexico on Navajo Land. It was a dry, windy, warm day. We drove many miles in a Chevy Blazer over dusty dirt roads. I was accompanied by a Captain from the Navajo Police Department, the Executive Director of the Community Youth Center, and a youth caseworker who was responsible for getting me to the location. I was thinking that I would probably get lost if I drove here on my own. All I saw was the never-ending crisscrossing of dirt roads that looked the same. After two hours of driving we arrived at the Chapter House.

The high desert had a beauty all of its own. The earth was a soft red-brown in color and had a clean sweet smell. When you grabbed a handful the dirt, it slipped through your fingers like powdered chocolate. The sky was blue and clear and the clouds sat still like giant pillows. I felt lucky to be far away from the insanity of the city.

The presentation was going to be held in the Chapter House and approximately twenty adults and elders from the community were expected. People had already gathered for my presentation; I began speaking on gangs in Indian Country. During the middle of my presentation, in a non-threatening manner, an elderly man stood up and interrupted my talk. He wanted to know who I worked for. I proudly responded, "I work for myself... I do not work for anyone." I spoke with a bit of bitterness still left from my days in the probation department. He put his head down and shook it over my answer. I was a bit perplexed.

He looked at me and firmly said, "No! You work for the Creator." The way he delivered his message humbled me. His words chased my arrogance away and grounded my purpose.

I paused, and thought about his words and said humbly, "Yes, you are right. I do work for the Creator. Thank you."

The elder helped me put my work into perspective; I thought a lot about his words. I realized that I am not perfect; I make mistakes. And like everyone else, I often say the wrong things. I acknowledge that the work I am doing is demanding. I realize my real boss is the Great Spirit and I am stronger when my faith is connected. Whatever I do or say is a reflection of that understanding. The acceptance of this philosophy gave me an inner strength that has assisted me in surviving obstacles with youth and poverty-stricken neighborhoods.

Paternal Memories

On one occasion, I was in Navajo Land doing a series of workshops throughout the reservation. I spent three weeks working with youth, presenting for teachers, police departments, and community members. I had completed an intense schedule of workshops. I was exhausted and ready to go home.

On my last day, I was invited to attend a Powwow in Tsaile, Arizona. My friend Walter Jensen was the Powwow Coordinator. Walter and some of my other friends worked at the Diné College. I was enjoying the drumming and the dancing, but at the same time I was looking forward to going home to my family. I had been on the road for three weeks and was missing the comfort of private life. Then the Gourd Dancers entered the arena and my focus changed.

Gourd Dancers are war Veterans from World War II, the Korean War, the Vietnam War, and Desert Storm. As I was listening to the drums, I watched the men dance with their gourd rattles dressed in both Army fatigues and Native regalia. The drums reminded me of my father; I began to feel sadness. They looked like my dad. My heart felt pain that I had not felt for some time. There was heaviness in my chest as I thought of him. It seemed as though each drumbeat brought me closer to the emotions of his loss. I could see my father's spirit dancing among the Gourd Dancers.

During the middle of the Powwow, the Arena Announcer called my name and asked me to approach. I was introduced to the community and was formally thanked for working with the youth and families of Navajo Land. It was an honor to be publically recognized. He shook my hand and I went back to my seat with a feeling of accomplishment.

A lot has happened since that warm dusty day at the old gas station outside of Page, Arizona when destiny took me through an exciting journey through Navajo culture and spirituality. I traveled throughout the Navajo Nation sharing tools and strategies in redirecting youth violence. At first, I thought my participation would only benefit the tribes and communities. It did not take me long to realize, that for everything I taught them, they taught me something new as well. I will be forever grateful to my friends of the Navajo Nation.

CHAPTER 8 FOCUS

Interacting with hardcore gang members while incarcerated, is different from working with them on the streets, away from institutional structure. When incarcerated, youth are easier to approach and open to healing. The juvenile justice system provides an abundance of spare time to reflect, their minds and bodies are free from substance abuse, and in most cases you have their attention. Yet, in the street, the institutional leverage to motivate is gone. The only factors you can depend on are a foundation of respect, trust, and your word. These elements will protect you and facilitate your ability to effectively communicate, motivating these young people to do their best.

Chapter IX

CORE SELF-CONCEPT

FOR MOST OF MY life, staying athletically fit has been a priority. Karate, running, and other forms of exercise have not only helped my body remain strong, but have also helped clear my mind. For example, running has always been something I could do to help blow off steam and rid myself of stress. While my feet beat the pavement I learned to release my accumulated weekly stress through the act of running. This activity for most of my life has been an instrumental tool of finding balance in a world that is often out of balance. This experience taught me that running could become a healing resource for incarcerated youth. I integrated mountain running as a structured activity at Joplin Youth Center in Orange County, California.

This correctional facility sat in the middle of pristine wilderness, Mother Nature's most picturesque land. Located near the Cleveland National Forest, the property was fenced-off and protected from public access. The landscape was extremely scenic with many untouched hiking trails, yet it was seemingly ignored by everyone consumed at Joplin Youth Center. I was motivated by the beauty and set out to create a program that would open a window of healing, by taking the incarcerated youth out to connect with the wisdom of the land.

Most of the youth at facilities like Joplin are *street smart*. They are survivors of urban warfare and domestic turmoil and many parents were relieved when their gang affiliated children were in custody. In the least, parents felt that their children were safe while in custody and did not have to worry about their child's safety and welfare. On the other hand, gang members saw their own incarceration as a time-off from the violence and pressures of the street. This reality, this perception, contradicted the systemic intent of punitive action.

The majority of the kids in the facility were Latino youth, while others were African Americans, some Caucasians, and Asians as well. But they all had the ability to manipulate the kindness of a well-intentioned staff. I had to have a firm, but fair approach toward these young men at all times. They tended to respect people who were able to *stand on their own two feet*, to be firm in their convictions.

During my first week at Joplin, a staff member mistook me for a minor in custody. He asked another staff member why I was walking out of my area unsupervised. He was a bit embarrassed to know I was his co-worker. His response did not surprise me. In fact, I was prepared to deal with such reactions; this was the second time.

There were only a few Chicano probation staff members at Joplin and everyone found it difficult to believe that I had no gang affiliation and that I had never been in a gang. Therefore, it was of no surprise when I was met with false expectations and prejudged from both sides of the cultural spectrum. These perceptions demonstrated that we had a long way to go in regards to acceptance. People are often placed in limited cultural categories and it was something that was happening at Joplin. Even though I had to deal with cultural stereotypes, I looked forward to working there because the program had a therapeutic, healing approach.

Programs

Years back when I decided to join the probation department, I wanted to be an agent of change and Joplin was a place where this seemed to be happening. The *line-staff* at Joplin and transferred staff were individuals who seemed to care about the youth and were willing to develop a variety of programs. We had developed a program called *Sail for Life*, where the youth learned how to sail boats while taught team-building skills. Their final exam consisted of sailing from Catalina Island together as a team. We also had a program on parenting for young fathers. Detailed, but simplified, we ran an institutional leadership program whereby privileges could be earned by participants making positive choices. Such privileges included working with handicap children at schools outside of the facility and weekend furloughs.

While at Joplin, I developed two programs, one of which was working with gang youth. I did not call it a "gang program" because I learned from past experience that the title would attract the negative element of gang behavior. I called it MAP: the Motivational

Awareness Program. It focused on bringing more of the cultural element to the youth. I invited guest speakers: community organizations, grieving mothers, positive role models, business people, public figures, and actors. One of our featured speakers was Victor Villaseñor, the acclaimed Mexican American author of the New York Times bestseller novel, *Rain of Gold*. I felt it was important to keep the youth connected to the outside world and have the opportunity to meet positive role models.

Mountain Running

Another program I coordinated was cross-country running. I had a similar program at Youth Guidance Center with obvious limitations. But at Joplin, running was ideal because of the steep trails and unused dirt roads. I loved the freedom and the unstructured time away from the facility.

I took five to ten youth running before breakfast, during week days and on weekends. Another co-worker would take them out on my days off. I developed a routine: I would arrive earlier for my morning shifts to prepare and then I would wake up the boys who were my loyal running companions. These young men loved taking part in this morning ritual while the entire camp was sleeping.

I found that it is important to be consistent with young men and to maintain a set routine. I knew that with time they would adapt and make it part of their everyday schedule. As a result, once solid positive habits were integrated, changes in their attitudes began to appear.

Often, after waking up early for a brisk mountain run, we would catch a glimpse of a deer gliding through the thick bushes. It was a sight of true art to see the swiftness and strength of a deer running effortlessly. I suggested they observe the running style of the deer and taught that a well-developed runner was someone who had the ability to glide like one. I would remind the young men to be as quiet as possible when running, that way they could see more of the wildlife.

Developing a trusting relationship with the young men was truly up to me. In order to do this I would have to be consistent with my actions and flexible with my time. Once gained, this trust has to be taken care of and maintained. If I were inconsistent, they would become inconsistent as well. My runners were aware that I was going beyond my duties with the extra activities for the running program. They knew I was not obligated to take them running every morning, but did it because I knew it was empowering for all of us, and I enjoyed it as well. They showed their appreciation; trust and respect grew from there.

Most of the youth who were in the program developed a healthy sense of humor and were mentally resilient from the months of training: of waking up early and running through steep mountain trails. My intent was to teach about *mental toughness*, to be able to resist the problematic addictions. I believe mental toughness is an important tool for young men to incorporate into their lives. It was my hope that this training would help them stay off drugs, out of jail, avoiding a criminal and violent lifestyle. After all, running is a unique and silent teacher.

I noticed that when the young men dedicated themselves to the training, they would learn about discipline and discovered their physical potential. They became skilled in dealing with stress while gaining knowledge and mental resiliency. Throughout the program, they were learning to develop both survival and coping skills.

Armando: A Case Study

One youth who excelled was Armando. He loved to go on runs and was usually the first one ready. Each morning I would find him patiently waiting by the staff desk area speaking with the solitary night staff or stretching near his bunk. He was the first one ready with a smile on his face, eager to hit the trail. Armando won several cross-country race competitions held with other youth correctional institutions.

Armando loved my program. Part of it was to run in community 5Ks and 10Ks or to participate in race competitions with other youth correctional facilities. Because of the sense of trust I had acquired with my runners, I never had an escape attempt during our community-sponsored runs or any other time.

Armando was in both of my programs and on my caseload, spending a lot of time with him. Continuously in trouble for fighting, he had a temper and was a skilled street fighter, not always a healthy combination. When he first arrived at Joplin he was on formal behavioral restriction. It took a month for Armando to transition to the environment. But once he got involved in positive activities, his behavior changed for the better. Armando was a natural in sports and loved baseball and most of the time he just needed guidance and direction.

Unfortunately, with all of his worthy attributes, he could not escape his past. He had been an active gang member with a history of drug addiction. He was a natural leader inside the institution and was frequently selected to fulfill leadership roles. He was articulate and knowledgeable about different subjects and he was eager to learn. Within a six-month period he had read over twenty college-level books and wrote reports on each, all for a soda and a snack.

I had developed a high level of trust with him. I was inspired by his intelligence and his eagerness to create a better life. He was on my caseload for almost a year and did everything I requested. I knew with the proper guidance, he could go far and eventually utilize his story and background as an asset, sharing his story as a source of inspiration to many youth with similar situations. Armando had a harsh background with physical violence at home, intense gang involvement, and time in and out of juvenile institutions as well as substance abuse issues. However, I believed in him. At that point in his life I considered him at a crossroads, where he would have to decide whether he wanted a healthy positive future, or a life of crime.

Armando was released from Joplin Youth Center after serving close to a year. I invited him to take part in my *Beyond Limits Program* which I continued to do during my vacation hours and time-off. He was motivated to take part in our adventures and participated in many excursions. In fact, during another trek up Mt.

Whitney, he and the other young men wanted to push themselves and break a *Beyond Limits* record for hiking up to Mt. Whitney. They wanted to backpack eighty-two miles from Sequoia National Park to Mt. Whitney in less than six days.

The group that was about to take the challenge consisted of five youth, a friend Hernan Pinilla and me. Hernan is a well-know musician from the South American band *Huaycaltia*. He was also in great condition from playing a lot of soccer and jogging on the weekends. We were more experienced and had invested a lot of training to take this challenge and all of us were in excellent shape. We had trained and were even more experienced than previous youth groups in the program.

I soon discovered that Armando was a robust backpacker with an independent swift pace. Because of his relentless pace, our strongest backpackers could not keep up with him, as he was averaging three hours in front of the entire group. He hiked like a seasoned backpacker with a bright smile and fast pace. When we arrived to the designated camp after a day of hiking, Armando had set up camp and taken a nap.

What I enjoyed about Armando was that he was unassuming about his abilities. He was helpful and added to the positive energy of the group. We completed that excursion in only five-and-a-half days. No one could believe our accomplishment; even I could not believe it. It was a very proud moment for us. I wanted the young men to be aware of their monumental success: this was an excellent example of what was possible when they set their minds on a goal.

The incredible part of this trip was that it was something the young people were motivated to accomplish. This excursion was run on automatic, everyone understood their responsibilities and I didn't have to talk to anyone regarding their behavior or remind them of what needed to get done. They were much more organized and mentally prepared than adults I had taken on similar trips.

Moving Away from the Madness

When I was invited back to the Navajo Nation, I took Armando with me. He had developed a rapport and empathy for many of the people there. We returned several times for speaking engagements; Armando became one of our main youth speakers. He was always articulate and had the ability to move people. Armando was a natural at public speaking. He usually received a favorable reaction from his audience when he shared his testimony.

The folks in Navajo Land saw the same positive qualities I saw in Armando. He was an effective speaker and made many friends and contacts with educators in the school district and throughout the community. A few months after the last trip to Navajo Land, Armando asked to speak with me. He indicated that he was ready to make more changes in his life. He had made a decision to move in with his older sister, a safe middle-class neighborhood in Moreno Valley, far from his previous gang activity. I supported his decision to move.

He would call me on a weekly basis to share the details of his new life. Armando had made the high school varsity football team earning the position of first string, defensive line. He received a *Good Citizenship Award* for his behavior and school attendance, and made the Academic Honor Roll that year. His senior year was special for him; it was the only normal school he had attended since being out of custody. By the end of the year, he had made new friends who were normal middle-class kids, and his football team won the city championship. Armando had completed a year of living a positive drug-free and gang-free life. I was proud of him.

Diné College

After graduating from high school, I met with him at his sister's house in Moreno Valley. He disclosed that he was ready for the next step. He wanted to go to junior college but wanted to move somewhere, far away. I was impressed with his commitment to having a better life.

I asked, "How about Navajo Land?" I told him that we have people over there that can help him get into the college and find employment. "You can go to Diné Community College and live in the dorms... I have contacts that could help." I had friends who worked and lived in the area. I told him that this was an opportunity for him to start building his life, and to heal from the negative experiences of his youth. "What do you think?"

He was silent for awhile and then replied, "Well, there is nothing here for me, and since I graduated, there is nothing to do... I will do it!"

I helped him obtain all the necessary paperwork for his first year of college. He was going to move hundreds of miles from home, to a different state with a different culture, far from the city. He was only eighteen. I continued believing in him. Armando had many admirable qualities; he was capable of handling himself on the street in dangerous situations. He was intelligent and had a natural charisma. People enjoyed talking to him.

However, his downfall was his addiction to drugs, his anger, and gang affiliation. Even though he was progressing, I knew his emotional pain was deep and if a certain unresolved trauma was not addressed, it would slowly manifest in negative behavior. I had seen numerous situations where people, who had not resolved their trauma, progressed and then slipped back into their negative habits. Overall, I was pleased Armando had decided to change his life's path. I felt Navajo Land and leaving the insanity of the inner city was the way to offer great opportunities to this young man who had become a big part of my life.

Diné College is located at the northeast tip of Arizona. The college is situated in the town of Tsaile, Arizona. The high desert there is amazing. The rich orange-brown earth is abundant with vibrant juniper trees and Arizona sagebrush sprinkled in the landscape. From the college, one can see the colorful Chuska Mountains that separate Arizona from New Mexico. In those days, we used to drive over the mountains to New Mexico on dirt roads. The mountains and area around the college would be a healthy experience for Armando, an opportunity that many people could only dream about.

I was told that Diné Community College was the first Native American College in the United States. During the mid-nineties it was called *Navajo College*. First opened in 1968, a tribally controlled community college. Set on Native American Land with a solid Diné architectural design. At the time, there were eight fifteen-room dormitories for about 150 students. The nearest town, Chinle, is about twenty-five miles away.

Not only was Armando going to live in an area that was naturally pleasing to the eye and lungs, but also filled with people who were spiritually and culturally rich. Navajo People have their stories, teachings, and healers that have been preserved and perpetuated for many years and the entire experience of attending this college would add to Armando's healing. I felt the experience, at a bare minimum, would be a solid reference point of what was possible for him.

Armando was ready; he packed up his clothes and school supplies. We left early Saturday morning before sunrise driving more than twelve hours. He was embarking on a new life at Diné College, in Northeast Arizona, a long way from his neighborhood. He quickly adjusted to his schedule.

During his first semester he made a lot of friends, he connected with his professors and excelled in his studies. I would often visit him when I was working in the surrounding area. He would call me every other week when I was at home. When I was in the area, I would take him with me to ceremonies, spend time with him and buy him the basic supplies he needed for school and survival.

144

Because of his motivation, he was asked to be a gang consultant for the Chinle School District in Navajo Land. He worked part-time at the Chinle School District Curriculum Office developing an approach to dealing with the gang problems in the town because many youth were getting involved with gangs. Influences came from Phoenix, California, and Chicago, and some of the Navajo youth had been developing their own style of gang activity.

With gangs come drugs, alcohol, and violence. The gangs on the Navajo Land were not at the level of the big cities, but they were growing. I believe that whenever you have youth who are not getting the love they need or proper guidance they crave, the negative element of life becomes more tempting. When this happens, they become more vulnerable to the negative side of life. Such negativity often consumes their lives and of the ones in their immediate circles. That is why what Armando was doing was important. He had first-hand knowledge of what is needed for a kid to avoid such a negative lifestyle.

I was periodically given reports by Armando's superiors that he was doing excellent work at his job. One of his supervisors went out of her way to help him. She took him on vacation trips with her family and was positive influence on him. Armando had that ability, to attract people into his life who were extremely supportive. Armando continued working for the Chinle School District while in school.

During this period, he had developed a romantic relationship with a Navajo woman, Deanna. She had a strong will and would not tolerate immature behavior. Deanna came from a traditional Navajo family, stable and loving. After several months they had taken him in as part of their family and he was able to move in with them. He seemed to get along well with her family, especially her father, a man of few words. Her father had his own business selling horse hay. Navajo people are hard workers and her father was an example of the Navajo work ethic.

Fortunately, Mexican culture has that same values and Armando was an attentive, hard worker, never having to tell him twice to do something. The father spent a lot time with Armando gathering wood in the mountains, hauling hay, and selling it in Chinle. The two developed a healthy father/son relationship. Everything in his life seemed to be going well.

Relapse

After a year of living in Navajo Land, Armando's phone calls became fewer and fewer. I thought he was just busy with school and his girlfriend. I received a phone call from a contact that worked at the college and he informed me that Armando was drinking and maybe using drugs, not attending his classes. He told me that someone needed to talk to him before things worsened. I decided to drive to the college that weekend since I was scheduled to conduct several workshops in the general area.

I drove twelve hours to see Armando, arriving tired, but eager to deal with the situation. I knew if I let it go, it would get worse. I was not angry; I was more disappointed and needed to hear Armando's side of the story. During the drive I kept thinking about how he was treading in dangerous territory; a relapse could be fatal. More than likely, I knew that recovering from a relapse would mean he would have to start all over with school, his job, and with the people who supported him the most.

I drove into the college parking lot at 5:30 a.m. Once out of the car, I took a deep breath and scanned the panoramic setting in the majestic Chuska Mountains, the picturesque land around the college. I loved the pristine high desert. It was early spring time and the weather was still chilly. Standing there, I remembered all the gatherings we had with the *Beyond Limits* and Navajo youth. The memories evoked a longing for that time.

The cold brush of air reminded me of why I was there. I wobbled into Armando's dorm area and knocked on his door. He opened the door and was shocked to see me. His thick hair was sticking up and he had pillow marks imprinted on the right side of his face. He seemed to be in shock. I had apparently awakened him up from a deep sleep.

I said to him in a direct, but tired voice, "What's going on Armando?"

"Nothing, Louie… just kicking it… What are you doing here?" He asked, surprised.

"Armando, get dressed we need to talk!" I said in a slightly frustrated tone. Pulling him out of his dorm room reminded me of when I used to go running with him and the other guys at Joplin Youth Center. Many changes had occurred since those two years and many more were to come if he did not clean up his life right then and there.

Armando and I sat there in the middle of the dorm room. He was wearing basketball shorts with no shoes or socks, with a T-shirt cut off around the deltoid area that displayed a small tattoo on his muscular brown arm. Armando went to the restroom and tried to manage his messy thick hair. I watched him wash his face with cold water. He then sat with me in the dorm visiting area.

I sat there staring at him, mentally picking my words and evaluating my approach to best help him. I did not want to push him too hard where he would shut down. I had to talk to him in a way that would bring about reflection. Armando mentioned that he was surprised to see me; I ignored his remark.

"Why are you using?" I asked. He just put his head down.

"I don't get it!" I told him. "Why are you using? Look, you can't use… you have an extensive history with drugs and alcohol. You know where that is going to take you! You have worked hard to stay away from all that madness."

He put his head down and a tear slid down his face. He partially covered his face with his hands as a form of frustration.

"You want to know why I am using?"

"Yes."

"I am using because people around here treat me like I am special! Like I am some sort of celebrity."

"Armando you are special. You have come a long way with your healing, you just don't see it. And you are going to throw it all away if you don't take care of yourself."

"I am not special, Louie!"

"What do you mean?"

He paused, took a deep breath and said, "I have done some fucked up things in my life! I have hurt people! And if people knew what I have done they would not treat me like they do!"

148

"You don't know that, Armando!" I said, interrupting him. "Where does your thinking come from? How does a person start thinking this way…? I want to know. Where did that come from? When did it start? "

He put his head down and thought about it, crossing his hands. He then lifted his head with slightly watering eyes, and said, "It came from my dad beating me as a little boy… it came from people telling me I am stupid and good for nothing. The schools and probation facilities told me I am a failure! They said I would never amount to anything… That's where it came from!"

"Where is that way of thinking going to take you?"

Without hesitation, he said, "It's going to take me to prison or I am going to end up dead." His responses to my questions were honest and took me aback.

I knew Armando had to redirect his drug abuse or it was going to take him back to the madness he had worked to avoid. We had many conversations that weekend. I took him with me to visit several Diné families I knew. We talked about his plans and what he needed to do to get focused with school and to stay sober.

After my work was complete, I told Armando I was going to return in two weeks. I was invited to speak at a conference at Page, Arizona with the renowned writer Luis Rodriguez. Luis had written several books on gangs, best known for his book *Always Running*. Armando had read it so I invited him to join us at the conference.

Two weeks later I picked up Luis Rodriguez at the high school in the town of Kayenta; from there I took him to Tsaile. We were able to spend the night at the college. We rented rooms in a hotel/dorm area. We picked up Armando the following morning at his girlfriend's parents house in Chinle. All three of us drove to Page, Arizona. We presented at the conference in the day and during the evening we took Armando out to eat at a Denny's restaurant, the only place open at that late hour. While at the restaurant, Armando shared with both us that he had made a decision to go back home to California.

"I don't think that is a good idea." I insisted. "You are not ready to be around the easy access to drugs and being around the gang element. You will make your situation worse. I think you should stay."

Luis Rodriguez echoed the same concern. He made reference to his background of gangs and drugs. Armando was stubborn. He smiled when I was talking to him. It looked as if he had already made a decision.

"If you won't give me a ride to California, I will take the bus. I am going home, my mind is made up. I miss my family." He said.

I figured he could ride with me and maybe I could talk some sense into him along the way. I was returning in a few weeks to do several workshops in Navajo Land and maybe I would be able to talk him into returning.

The following day after the conference, his girlfriend's family hosted a barbeque for him. Her entire family was there. The food was great. After the delicious meal, mostly her family members, stood up and shared their thoughts with Armando. Her family had given him their unconditional love. The entire family was trying hard not to show their sadness over the change in his nature and decision to leave. His girlfriend's father shared some direct encouraging words and then abruptly left the house to attend to his duties.

After the meal and cheerless goodbyes, we made our way to California. I had a positive conversation with Armando on the long drive back and I tried talking him into returning to Navajo Land. He assured me he would think about it. I dropped him off with his family.

Disconnection

After two months, Armando stopped returning my phone calls and began avoiding me. I went several times to his home and he was nowhere to be found. His mother told me nervously that she was worried and had lost faith in him. She mentioned that he had been better off in Arizona.

The last time I saw Armando was when I was asked by Terri, a family friend, to talk to him. This was around four months after I had driven him home. He had gotten deeper into the gang lifestyle and was using *crystal meth*. Everyone was worried. Terry invited me to her home and inadvertently invited Armando and his older brother without letting them know that I was going to be there.

I remember that it was a dark, windy and rainy evening. Nature was representing the gloomy situation we were experiencing. I drove across town to visit with him through stop-and-go-traffic and in heavy rain. I went into the house and some of his family members where there as well as Terri's family. I spoke with everyone, made myself comfortable, and waited for this young man who had become a big part of our lives.

LUIS R. RUAN

He came into the house with his brother. They were wearing baggy khaki pants, had shaved heads, and looked like your average gangsters. My heart hurt a bit seeing him in his old ways. I could tell he was *using* because of his negative edge, something in his behavior and in his eyes. When he came into the living room he sat down with his brother and began saying in a defiant manner, "I am tired of people telling me what to do. I know what I need to do and ain't nobody going to tell me how to do it."

With no expression on my face, I stood up and said goodbye to the family, and explained that I needed to be leaving. I thanked them for everything and stated that my work was done and that I needed to get home. I grabbed my jacket and headed for the door. The people who were present in the room understood what I was doing. I needed to creatively capture his attention.

"Hey Louie, where you going?" Armando asked me. He seemed confused.

"I am not needed here; you seem to have all the answers." I answered and continued saying good bye to Terri, the family, and to his brother. He looked at me blankly, "Let's talk outside before I leave."

Once outside, I noticed it had stopped raining. As we stood in front of the house he shared with me that his remark about being tired of being told what to do was not about me and that he was just tired of everyone on his back.

"You *were* talking about me," I told him. "I came over here to talk and to see how you are doing. That is my job, to let you know when you are going towards a cliff. I will always say something when you are hurting yourself. I do this for your own good, you know how I am. I have known you for many years and have always been honest with you. I still believe in you, I believe in your potential."

"But you have given up!" I continued. "You have chosen a way of life that will take you to the grave or behind bars. Is this what you want? I just want to tell you that I can't help you anymore."

Baffled he asked, "What do you mean, Louie?"

"I can't help you because you are not willing to help yourself! You are deep into your addiction and gangs. I can't help you. You have chosen this life that I do not support."

"What?" He asked.

I tried to be careful, but honest with my words, "You do not have the fire to overcome this, and I don't think you want to. When you are ready, call me. I will keep you in my prayers."

He came over to me, gave me a hug and left. I stood there watching him walk away, feeling powerless, and knowing this path would engulf his spirit. While it hurt me, I knew there was nothing I could do about it. It was his choice.

At that moment, I knew I would never see or hear from him again. Even so, I did not give up on him. I believe that people will always have the opportunity to change their lives for the better. It depends on the individual's willingness and their dedication to redirect themselves from the negative. The important factor was that Armando had many reference points of success and support. But he found that his drug addiction, thus his gang involvement, were not easy to escape. He left the unfamiliar idyllic surroundings, a loving community, and a promising future, to return to a dangerously familiar lifestyle.

Last I heard about Armando was that he was back in prison. I wrote to him a couple of times, and then I lost contact. During our last conversation he asked me to include his story in my book.

Core-concept

Looking back, I think that in Armando's case, as with many people, it comes down to how we see ourselves at a core level... the very essence of being. Going beyond the façade and confronting unresolved issues that lurk within.

On the surface, Armando was a handsome, athletic, confident and intelligent young man. However, within his core-concept he saw himself as an ugly person, unworthy of a fulfilling life, and incapable of healing his past. His trauma remained unresolved and his negative dialogue poisoned his success. No matter how much he accomplished, how far he was away from the city, that inner core self-concept would impede his development. It was like a solid spider web that suspended his development, healing, and any hope to do better.

His negative self-image was deeply embedded in his psyche. When we do not change our core-concept, we attract the mirror of those beliefs in the physical. That physical mirror will eventually manifest into a reality. Armando attracted the scenario that placed him in state prison.

I see people doing this all the time at different levels. We will attract those things that are ingrained in our being. An abundance of money, a new house, a new car, a physical makeover, a different geographical area, nothing will change if the core-concept is not altered.

CHAPTER 9 FOCUS

Core self-concept has to do with resolving deep core issues that impede our growth and development, the idea that we need to do the necessary work and accept that we are worthy of healing. If your clients do not believe they are worthy of healing, all the work in the world will not change their situation. Many times, people do a lot of external work but completely ignore doing the internal work. These issues are easily ignored because the internal work is much more intricate. Core self-concept brings to light the reality of true transformation; equal effort has to be placed in the internal and external shaping of one's transformation.

CHAPTER X

HEALING BROKEN WINGS

THERE WAS A TIME in my life when I was fortunate enough to inhabit two very different communities: Boyle Heights, an urban community of East Los Angeles where I worked, and Lake Forest, a suburban community in Orange County where I lived with my wife and two sons.

Lake Forest was a middle-class pre-planned community with aesthetically pleasant homes and many well-maintained parks, empty most of the time. I enjoyed living in Lake Forest because of the abundance of trees and the easy access to hiking trails where I frequently observed deer, bobcats, snakes, red tail hawks, and other animals. It was quiet, safe, clean, but lacked a sense of community as people lived their separate lives, disconnected from each other.

Boyle Heights, adjacent to the Los Angeles River and known by many as the gateway to East Los Angeles, maintained a vibrant cultural history. From the vendor pushing his Mexican ice cream cart calling out to the neighborhood kids, to the elderly lady smiling at passersby while waiting for her bus, Boyle Heights was a place where people *lived* and interacted. The people of Boyle Heights were very much alive and in constant interaction with one another. I felt safe and was honored to work there. I loved it so much that I was motivated to drive the more than ninety-mile commute.

Looking back, I'm so glad I did. During that time, I was working as a Youth Mentor Coordinator for the *Impacto* Program of *Proyecto Pastoral*, a Catholic faith-based nonprofit organization that was created by the residents of Boyle Heights and Jesuit priests. Even though I was not Catholic, I was permitted to work for *Proyecto Pastoral* and respected the agency's progressive and innovative approaches to empowering the community.

The Boyle Heights section of East Los Angeles was made famous by the activism of Father Greg Boyle who worked diligently assisting the community and its gang members. Since gangs had a heavy presence in the Boyle Heights community, Father Boyle decided to take on the challenge to help these young people choose different paths as well as provide supportive programs. "Father G," as he is known by many in Boyle Heights, has also seen the tragic side of working with troubled youth, having buried more gang members than any other priest in the United States.

I have always respected the social activism of the Jesuits who often work in the most uncertain areas of the world. Many work and live alongside people who have suffered and have been dismissed by society. In the Boyle Heights community, Father Boyle has earned a high level of admiration and support for his resourceful and encouraging endeavors.

Father Boyle is an example of putting God's work into action and being a dynamic agent of change. Anyone who works tirelessly to make a community safer and more self-sufficient is unique. Father Boyle, along with members from around his community, has worked to develop local businesses help countless gang members change their lifestyles. He instills a sense of dignity in these youth and adults by finding legitimate sources of employment for them. His programs, *Jobs for the Future*, and *Impacto* were two of many programs under the non-profit organization, *Proyecto Pastoral*.

In Boyle Heights, the average resident has to deal with a high level of environmental stressors associated with a lack of resources in an overpopulated area. There were/are very few employment opportunities for youth and effective after-school programs designed to keep teenagers productively engaged. Showing these young people that they could find jobs, despite their tattoos or gang affiliations, provided many with something they never had before: an option and encouragement to do something different with their lives.

When I worked there, it was a common occurrence to hear gunshots from my office, sometimes from a distance, and occasionally nearby. One day while we were conducting a support group for high-school youth, someone from the street shot at our building and hit a window pane. Although the bullet was not intended for a specific person at our agency, the residual bullet hole in the window taking months to repair was a topic of conversation, a reminder of the harshness that plagued the inner city streets.

One of the responsibilities I had in the *Proyecto Pastoral* was to recruit professionals who were willing to be mentors for at-risk elementary and middle school youth. It was my job to find effective role models who would be willing to make a commitment mentoring a child and see them through an entire year, actively participating in their lives. These mentors helped guide these troubled youth towards full participation in school and community activities. Most mentors surpassed the one year requirement, helping these kids through to high school. Everyone associated with the program found great satisfaction and sustained productive interaction. It reminded me of the importance of mentoring as a vital component in redirecting misguided youth.

Story of the Eagle and the Hawk: A Pivotal Experience
I was in my office at *Impacto* on a typical East LA mid-summer day when I experienced a spiritual awakening, now integrated into my worldview; it gave me perspective…

I had spent most of the afternoon meeting with the program director, Francisco Chavez in his office area. Never in my life had I worked with a director who was so engaged in improving the conditions of a community.

Francisco was born and raised in Boyle Heights and was once an active gang member; he did his share of jail time. Then in his early twenties, he decided to change his life. He managed to go to college, earn two Master's Degrees, and teach at the university level.

After teaching at several universities, he volunteered three years of his life as a member of the *Sandinista National Liberation*

Front and fought in the jungles of Nicaragua. Following his tour of duty, he moved to Los Angeles and accepted a job as the director of the *Impacto* Program. All of his previous experiences allowed him to have a compassionate, committed, disciplined, and unifying approach to working within the community.

During this meeting with Francisco, one of our summer workers, a teenager named Annabel from the Pico-Aliso Neighborhood Projects, barged into the meeting and said, "Louie, you have a phone call from *Señora* Lupe... she said it is important."

At the same time, Francisco's phone rang. While he talked to his boss, I looked outside the window of his air-conditioned office and thought about how lucky I was to be indoors. The summer heat was uncomfortably humid and it felt as if the sun's force was purposefully cooking the neglected weathered streets and sidewalks. This heat wave was intensified by the scarcity of trees, a nonexistent breeze, and the lack of open space around Boyle Heights. It seemed as if the over-crowded community created more heat and intensity. Impatiently, Annabel reminded me of my telephone call, "Louie! She is still waiting on the phone."

"Tell her I will call her back... I am busy," I mumbled.

Annabel in her strong, melodic East LA accent, with her hands on her hips and her head tilted in defiance, chewing a wad of gum, "She said it is an emergency, eh."

I explained to Francisco that I had better speak with her because it sounded important. I walked over to my office to speak with *Señora* Lupe. I picked up the phone and said, "Yes Lupe, how can I be of service?" She explained in a rushed tone how a person selling rare exotic birds had offered to sell her an eagle. Lupe explained how she believed the eagle was being mistreated by the seller. The eagle was being sold for $150. She asked me if I was willing to help her out with part of the money. I told her I would get back to her before I went home. I spoke with my director, and even though we did not know what this bird looked like, we decided to buy the so-called eagle.

Señora Lupe worked at the agency on the next block across the street from my office. She was a warm, quick-witted, resourceful, middle-aged Mexican woman who had experienced her share of life's challenges.

I knew her because she facilitated parenting classes for the parents whose children were enrolled in our program. Her workshops consisted of teaching parenting skills and empowering the families to become better parents. The majority of our parents loved her workshops. *Señora* Lupe was able to instill a sense of hope in her classes. She was humble and had a survivor's sense of humor. She was also an aficionado of rare birds.

Francisco and I pitched in together to buy the eagle; we jokingly asked Lupe: "Are you sure it isn't an overfed chicken from the projects?" I was skeptical because I knew the majority of folks in the East Los Angeles area have never seen an eagle. I mean, we are lucky if we see the stars at night! Over the years, I had seen red-tailed hawks in certain areas of East Los Angeles, but never an eagle. The only reason I had a rough knowledge of eagles was because of my travels and work throughout Native American Reservations.

According to Lupe, the bird had been tied up and mistreated by its owner. We bought the bird with the intent of saving it from more mistreatment. The three of us never thought twice about our decision to save the bird.

The next day *Señora* **Lupe** called and asked us to meet at her office. When I arrived Lupe had the bird in an old metal black cage. She was sitting on the floor, feeding the bird through the cage. Lupe talked to it as if it were a lost relative from out-of-town. It was apparent that she had an enormous amount of compassion for the bird. As she was feeding it, I heard bird sounds in the background in her office on an old radio cassette player. For a minute, I thought I was in a bird sanctuary. She told me the recorded sounds would make the bird feel at home. I think it made *her* feel more at home.

When I looked at the bird, I realized the bird was a hawk, not an eagle. I glanced at the hawk and diplomatically told her, "Lupe, this is not an eagle, it is a hawk."

She looked at me with a bewildered facial expression, and quickly responded in Spanish, "Oh well, it is still beautiful and precious..." then turned toward me and asked, "What should we do with it? We have nowhere to put it... if we return it, the bird will be mistreated and sold on the black market."

Not sure what we could do, "Let's sleep on it and talk about it tomorrow."

Before I went home for the day, I took one last look at the hawk. It gazed at me intently with its piercing dark eyes; it seemed to look right through me. I could feel its power and felt as if it could catch a glimpse of my soul. I had never been eye-to-eye with a hawk before, and this bird got into the core of my being. Perhaps, it was because it was still wild and pure, or maybe because it had an innate connection to nature and survival. Most of the hawks I have seen in the Zoo were institutionalized and wore a beaten and defeated look. This hawk was connected to the cycle of nature and had been free. We fed it and watched it just ripped through the raw meat with its sharp talons and beak. After devouring its meal, the hawk tried to spread its huge wings and fly. I saw the hawk hit its head and exhibit frustration at being in a strange, foreign, confining environment.

The next morning, after much discussion between the three of us, we decided not to return it to the, *so-called* original owner, who would only try to domesticate it and treat it poorly. We all knew the bird did not belong in a cage. It was out of its natural world. It was apparent from the way the hawk hit its head and wings against the cage that the bird had a difficult time accepting the restrictions of its captivity. We agreed that I would take the bird to the mountains and let it go. The hawk needed an environment where it could soar, where it could be unrestrained among the elements.

The next day I left the office by 5:30 p.m. This is peak traffic time in Los Angeles and I found myself driving on the 5 North bound Freeway headed towards the Angeles National Forest, the closest natural mountain environment to Los Angeles.

During the drive, the hawk kept hitting its head and trying to fly inside the cage. Within minutes, the smell of the bird was difficult to endure with my windows rolled up. To add to the tension, the L.A. traffic was typical, stop and go. I could see in my rear view that the hawk continued his attempt to escape. The situation created a high level of apprehension for me and my passenger. I drove with the hawk in the back of my jeep for more than an hour.

When we arrived in the Angeles Forest, the sun was slowly making its descent. I was finally away from the stress of rush hour traffic. I could no longer hear the clatter and hollow sounds. I was glad to arrive in a sanctuary of melodious bird echoes and the fresh scent of the earth.

Once in the forest, I searched for a clearing away from where other people were likely to pass. I hiked up a grassy knoll with the cage in my hand. I heard the sounds of birds and found an area where I could pray. I lit a coal, and burned flat cedar on the hot charcoal; I blessed the hawk with the smoke of the cedar and recited a short prayer. After a few minutes, I opened up the cage and told the bird to go home. The bird did not seem to understand that the cage was opened and just stood there frozen, appearing traumatized and confused. It just stared back at me with piercing eyes.

The hawk would not keep its eyes off of me. I bumped the back part of the cage with the palm of my hand, to provoke the hawk to move forward. Gradually it wobbled out and continued to stare at me with a look of confusion and still would not leave. I sprinted towards the frightened hawk with my hands up high to make it fly away. As it flapped open its wings, I saw how much bigger they were in flight. It flew on top of a large oak tree, and then it vanished into the mountain landscape. The hawk was finally at home in the wilderness.

Driving back home in my Jeep, the unbearable aroma of the hawk permeated my car. The hawk had mixed its food and waste inside the cage. The smell was pungent. As I continued driving, my thoughts flowed into a reflection of what this experience represented in my life. I instantly began to see images of all the young men and women who had crossed my path who were in juvenile facilities, prison, addicted to drugs, and the ones who were no longer with us in the physical world. Many of these young people had lived a life without obtaining their human potential, dismissing their innate gifts that would have provided them all with a more fulfilling life.

All the way home, the experience reminded me of the people who are imprisoned behind invisible bars, individuals who are held back by their addictions, domestic violence, or involvement with gangs. I even thought about those who were imprisoned by their own internal fears.

Such unresolved trauma and the fear it creates truly impact one's potential. I have seen countless young men and women who had the ability to be leaders, maybe a future accountant, a therapist, an engineer, or artist, without the resources to reach their potential or dream. Many of the youth, who came into my mind during that reflective moment, were not able to experience their capabilities and gifts. This is the sad reality of what happens to human beings when the conditions around them are disabling. They are like the hawk in the cage.

I know the Great Spirit did not create us to be imprisoned. Like the hawk, we were meant to be free and to soar and to live a meaningful and fulfilling life. For some individuals, a prosperous life comes easily; others have to sacrifice and work hard. Our dreams are all attainable, no matter where we are in life. Regardless of our background and experience, a harmonious life is possible.

◎ ◎ ◎

Solitary Confinement

Sometime later, I shared this hawk story with my friend Alex who was incarcerated in Corcoran State Prison serving a ten year sentence. He had been incarcerated for long periods of time since he was an adolescent in Los Angeles. He was only twenty-seven, and found himself in prison again.

Alex, who was involved in gangs, had gang and prison tattoos all over his body, some covering his entire shaved head. I would look at his tattoos and imagine how his body looked like a clean canvas before he walked into a facility. Now, he was a mural of experience. I think if I had not known him through several years of correspondence, and just saw him on the street, I would have been too intimidated to talk to him. The thing about Alex was that he had an apparent physical presence, like the captain of a college football team, or a brave, high-ranking officer in the military. He had a noticeable warrior spirit, but due to his environment and some poor choices, he unfortunately ended up in the California Penal System.

While Alex was sincere and internally strong, he was also the epitome of a hardened prison Chicano gang member. He was a survivor of the California prison system's most grueling environments. Like many other young men with similar backgrounds, he excelled in the streets and within the prison culture; he was a gangster. His upward mobility was similar to that of a successful Wall Street Executive – wily, manipulative, but charming when he wanted to be.

When I met him, he was in the Special Housing Unit, the SHU. This unit is also referred to as *solitary confinement* or *the hole*. While in the SHU, he decided to change his life. I worked with him because I saw his authenticity. I would often write to Alex and send him stories I wrote to get his feedback. I sent him a rough description of the experience I had with the hawk in Boyle Heights.

He replied in a letter where he wrote his thoughts, "Louie that is me... I am that caged bird. When I get released, I have no idea how to act or how to function because I am so institutionalized. I am scared! "

I have counseled numerous ex-cons, and found that the transition from prison to the world outside is difficult. There are few transitional programs while in prison. Some people have no sympathy: "Well, they're ex-cons...Who cares?" Such people need to realize the chance of an ex-prisoner's success is based on outside support and preparation beyond the prison walls.

Upon release, each inmate is given $200 dollars to survive. Often, the parole officers are so over-worked that they are not able to find adequate job training or employment for ex-cons. I have witnessed what happens with ex-cons during job interviews, and the truth is that nobody wants to hire somebody with tattoos and a prison record.

Another major obstacle to the success of prison inmates is the lack of a positive relationship with family and friends. Often, these men and women do not have family to assist them. Sometimes they have burned all their bridges. That is why transitional and sober living homes are vital for the survival of someone who has been released from prison. If they become adjusted and do well in society, everyone benefits on many levels: *the liability becomes an asset.*

When a human is incarcerated for a long period of time, they become institutionalized. They are used to being fed three meals a day and solve their problems with others through violence and manipulation. Becoming un-institutionalized takes time and patience. Unfortunately, some ex-cons find prison life is easier than to live on the outside, so they find ways to break the law, get caught, and return to prison.

I share the story of the hawk because it is important that we identify our limited thinking and our limited patterns. I know many people who have been traumatized by life and have become imprisoned by their experiences. What is helpful is to go through the healing process and not prolong the healing by denying the pain. We need to walk through the pain in order to heal from it. Doing this takes bravery and support from the people who care about us. When we heal, we are able to walk through life with a healthy and fulfilling attitude. We can be rich or poor and still be in balance and harmony.

Wings of the Eagle

Once, I was backpacking in Southern Colorado on the Ute Reservation with an inner city youth group. We were about to begin a long, strenuous hike when suddenly, a beautiful full-grown golden eagle soared twelve feet above crossing the trail. I was struck by the eagle's elegance and perfection as it flew effortlessly beyond the horizon. Its golden-brown wings spanned seven feet. In a matter of seconds, the majestic image of the eagle made its way to the other side of the mountain. I stood there on that dusty trail with my group as we marveled at the splendor of the golden eagle. The aesthetic image has remained in my mind and soul.

Ancient cultures have always attentively observed nature as a way of understanding the complexities of life. All animals, insects, seasons, trees, and plants have something to teach us. Many aspects of the eagle can be used as life teachings that are practical and enlightening. The experience with the hawk reminded me of the teachings of the eagle.

The eagle is able to fly higher than most birds. For Native people throughout most of the Americas the eagle is a symbol of sacredness and a physical connection to the Great Spirit. The eagle is one of my favorite animals. This majestic bird has numerous profound and practical teachings.

1. *The eagle gives us a model for healthy, developed relationships.*
   The eagle keeps one mate for life; it makes a full commitment and sticks to it.
2. *Look seven times further at a situation before making major decisions.*
   The eagle has incredible eyesight; it can see and distinguish objects with a vision seven times more powerful than human vision.
3. *When life gets difficult and we feel threatened we should move toward the light – with spirituality and faith.*

The eagle, with its second eyelid, has the ability to fly away toward the sun (light) when attacked.

4. *With hard work and belief in ourselves, we can go through life with grace, respect, dignity, and wisdom.*

   The eagle is gifted with two very agile wings. The left wing symbolizes *hard work;* the right wing represents *belief.* Both wings work in harmonious synchronization. This natural harmonious effectiveness with the two wings empowers the eagle to fly higher than any bird, to fly with dynamic speed and precision.

A Human Eagle: Samuel's Story

When I worked in one of the probation camps as a counselor I met an inmate, Samuel. Over six feet tall, slim, and consumed with deep-seated anger toward the world, he was very belligerent and ready to fight anyone at a moment's notice. When I first met him he was squaring off with staff members. Several of the deputies were over six feet tall and each a hundred pounds heavier with solid muscle. Samuel was tall and skinny, with no apparent athletic muscle mass. What made the situation worse was that the deputies were getting very impatient with Samuel's behavior.

I heard him verbally assaulting a staff member, provoking him to fight with his hands. Saying, "Come on! I will take you right now! You ain't shit, man!"

I was afraid this young probation officer was going to fall into Samuel's trap. Fortunately, some of the more experienced staff were able to intervene and calm Samuel and the officer down. Samuel was sent back to juvenile hall for his behavior and placed in a unit that had much more structure.

After three months, he returned to the probation camp and placed on my caseload. Surprisingly, he was much calmer and did not have that belligerent energy as before. He had earned extra time because of his excessive fighting; now serving a year sentence. As I grew to know him, I learned that Samuel was an extremely intelligent young man. He excelled in school and loved to read. I would bring many books about history, culture, and spirituality. We also had great conversations about his background and his future. During one of our conversations, he asked what I thought about faith.

I shared with him about the power of prayer and the importance of supporting our prayers with action. He asked me to explain it a little more. I shared with him, that if we prayed every day – morning, afternoon, and evening – and had faith in those prayers, it would manifest in God's time. We talked about this topic for an hour.

For the next five months he would kneel down on his bunk and bowed his head to pray. He did this ritual three times a day. The other kids just left him alone and allowed him to pray, free from ridicule. After five or six months of consistent prayer and faith, he was called into the main office to speak with my supervisor. A new program was implemented to alleviate the over-crowding in the juvenile institutions and they were releasing minors to house arrest. On house arrest, minors spend most of their time in their homes and are not allowed to go to school. It was a better deal than being in a structured probation facility.

Samuel approached my desk with a perplexed look on his face, "I am getting released tomorrow. My grandmother is going to pick me up..."

"So what is the problem?" I asked him.

"I just can't believe it. I can't believe that I am going home tomorrow morning." He said as he sat on his bunk with his arms covering his chest like a blanket.

"Samuel, Samuel!" I said, trying to get him out of his shock. "This is what you wanted, isn't it? You prayed for this and you got it. You need to say thank you to whoever you prayed to."

Samuel was released to his grandmother and never returned to a probation facility. He would call every three months to update me on his progress. He had applied the idea of having faith, but he also did the necessary work to make things happen in his life.

Using Your Left Wing

The eagle's left wing represents hard work and the ability to take precious action in order to create change. Sometimes, people dream about change, but refuse to do the actual work. After Samuel made a decision to alter his life, he applied himself to improving his situation inside and outside the institution. He did the work by being open to change. Samuel asked for help from all the probation staff. Samuel applied what he learned from the positive influence of the adults who supported him. He enrolled in all the programs that were available to help him. He volunteered for jobs inside the institution that kept his mind and body occupied. Because of his efforts, he earned the trust of the staff and was in a better place mentally and emotionally. Doing the work is imperative, and only complements the right wing, which represents belief.

Using Your Right Wing

The eagle's right wing represents belief or faith. By having faith, that does not mean you have to be religious. Instead, this means having a faith within, where we need to believe that our dreams will become a reality, what we believe will manifest, and healing is possible with the right dose of application. Yet many of the young people I have worked with throughout the years, did not believe they were worthy of a happy, harmonious life.

Work and belief are necessary for true healing to occur. Like the eagle and the hawk, both wings are needed to rise above situations. By flying, we can see our problems more clearly and from many angles. By rising above our hardships, we let go of those situations that have caused pain and have impeded happiness and balance. These two wings, working in synchronization, aid us in the ability to understand our destiny and purpose.

CHAPTER 10 FOCUS

The winged animals have much to teach us about how to live a long fulfilling life. The way of the hawk and eagle is opposite to the self-imposed mental obstacles that people embrace. This negative mindset is the most deceptive and difficult to understand. There are three levels of understanding that will assist in rising above any situation: The first is to acknowledge your reality. The second is to synchronize work and belief to attain transformational healing. The third level is to use your process and journey as a lesson for others who have parallel experiences.

CHAPTER XI

BASCO

WHEN I WORKED IN THE probation department I dealt with a lot of young people. In the Boyle Heights community, I was responsible for assigning mentors for the neighborhood youth. I was then asked to work directly with young adults by focusing on their community leadership development program. I did not mind wearing this new hat and I was excited to work with teens.

I easily transitioned into the youth program despite the many complications around it. The program was on a shaky foundation when I joined due to community dissatisfaction with previous administrative approaches. One dilemma that presented itself was that several of the youth felt the program was pushing an abrasive form of Latina feminism and Mexican Indigenous Native culture down their throat. They also felt that college educated outsiders were coming into their community and pushing their agenda without asking the youth what they wanted to learn.

On the other hand, there were youth who were involved with the previous program and were content with the former staff and feeling deeply disappointed when they left. They considered me an outsider although I had worked with the previous program assisting in the young men's support group. Because of these conflicts some of the previous staff voluntarily quit, moved on, or were fired. These prevailing issues created a distrustful relationship with the new adult staff and the youth that lived in the area. This was the challenge the new program we inherited.

These issues created a conflict between the two youth groups. The entire program had been at a standstill by all the conflicting opinions and feelings revolving around it. What stood out for me was that the staff was prepared for this. They had the key elements that were necessary for working with both groups: motivation, compassion, love and dependability. The staff enthusiasm was contagious and when we were together, we felt we could solve any problem.

The staff immediately formed new objectives to redirect the youth. The first step was to help heal past issues. The second was to develop trust. The third was to create a positive space. And lastly, we were to develop an operational leadership program that was run by the youth and their adult mentors. It has always been my philosophy that the youth should develop approaches to community involvement of their own accord. The adult's presence is to offer suggestions and to provide support that would guide participants to learn and to develop. While we felt ready to share our new goals and objectives, we knew we had to address the prevailing distrust the youth had toward the agency.

We decided to hold a meeting in our facility and invite any youth who was interested in getting involved with a new dynamic youth leadership program. It was agreed that my leadership curriculum was going to be used as a framework for the program. We spoke to several community workers in the neighborhood and asked them to put the word out that all youth were invited to take part in the *Impacto Youth Leadership Program.* The word on the street was that the youth felt resistant, but at the same time interested in what we had to say. Fortunately, we had several staff members, community volunteers, and community youth outreach workers who had an encouraging rapport with the Boyle Heights youth. We had hoped they would attend the meeting.

Staff

The staff for the new program was composed of individuals with interesting backgrounds that added to the richness of the agency:

The director of *Impacto* was Christine Sanchez. She had spent most of her career in the corporate world. Her positive work ethic and love for the youth was beneficial to running the program. She was also a solid leader.

Carlos Vasquez, an avid basketball player, managed the program with an ability to connect deeply with youth. He had great rapport and was well received by young people.   Alejandra Azucena, a college graduate in social work, was dedicated and passionate about working with youth; she had a sweet and compassionate disposition.

Dowrin Suarez, born and raised in the Aliso Projects, worked part-time and attended community college part-time. She was known for her patience, sense of humor, and a deep level of compassion for the youth.

Raul, "Rulies" Diaz who worked at another city youth program at the time, volunteered at *Impacto* as well. He was born and raised in the neighborhood. His family was responsible for creating positive outcomes through their activism. Whenever something major occurred in the community we would ask *Rulies* for details and guidance; he had the pulse of the community.

My role was to develop and implement my curriculum and teach music to the youth, guitar and Andean flute. The staff was phenomenal and a perfect match for the youth leadership program. We were ready to go!

The Meeting

Our first meeting was scheduled on a weeknight. We placed forty chairs in a circular formation and waited for the youth to arrive. The vibe in the air was heavy; most of us were nervous and anxious to get the program going. The youth began to slowly stagger into the building. Most of them had an appearance of mistrust as they circled the room and eventually found a safe place to sit. Several greeted us reluctantly and the few who had openly greeted us did so with youthful smiles. I recall Christine beginning the meeting by asking everyone to introduce themselves. After the introductions, one *Impacto* staff member stated our intentions for the program. Several of the staff emphasized that all we wanted to do was work with the youth in this community.

By the looks on some of their faces, the youth did not look particularly inspired by our positive attitudes. One lanky young man with Mexican indigenous appearance, dressed in *hip-hop* clothing with a baseball cap turned purposely to the left side of his head, scornfully asked, "What are you guys, trying to convince us... to be like Indians or what? This is *our* neighborhood!" He peered at me as if waiting for a response. He then turned away.

I smiled over the irony: this guy looked more Indian than I did and could go to any Native Nation and blend in like a local. There was a lot of anger and harsh words from the youth toward the agency and the adults. Since we represented the agency, we had to tolerate their harsh words and attempted to improve the negative image they had of us.

Another slender young man stood with anger splattering out with each of his words, "We don't want anybody telling us what to do and what to believe in! Are you staff going to be like the other group? Because if you are, you're all lame!" He sat down and crossed his arms in defiance.

I responded, doing my best not to allow my ego to speak, and shared with the group how we did not want to tell them what to do, that I did not want to make anybody a "born-again Indian."

All staff members took turns speaking to the group. We made it clear how we wanted to offer a space where they could visit and take advantage of resources that could benefit them. Christine, Rulies, and Carlos did a great job of articulating our intentions.

After an hour of arguing and accusations, Christine asked the question, "What can we do to heal the relationship between the youth, adults, and the agency?" They kept quiet, but I could see them communicating with each other with their eyes, around the room. I could tell that they were used to dealing with this type of confrontation. It seemed like no one had anything positive to say.

Then Leo spoke up and in a confident voice and said, "Maybe we can start by going on a retreat to the mountains, to get to know each other." He was charismatic and persuasive; he had a way with his peers. The other youth participants nodded their heads in agreement. One young man was still attempting to engage in an argument, but soon the hostility wore down and everyone was in agreement with Leo.

The staff organized a retreat for the following weekend. Everyone stayed in a secluded cabin, hidden in the mountains of Big Bear, California. The importance of the retreat was to show how the adult staff kept their word, and the youth were able to experience being in a relaxing environment in the California Mountains, away from the city stress. The youth and adults bonded and had a great time.

After a few months, we had more youth who wanted to be part of the program. It got to the point where the students did not want to leave the *Impacto* building and lingered even when it was time for the staff to go home. Within six months of the initial meeting, the trust between the youth and *Impacto* staff began to take root and the healing was in full force. For many of the teenagers, the program became a safe haven from the intensity of the streets. After school, the center would become crowded with the neighborhood teenagers.

◎ ◎ ◎

Youth Programs at Impacto

There were a variety of programs. We offered a leadership program, a college preparatory program, a theater group, and a music class that I facilitated. The first hour of the program consisted of making time for the youth to do their homework. During that hour, all staff assisted with the occasional help of volunteers from the local colleges.

While most days went by smoothly, there were occasions when the youth could not keep quiet during study hours. When that happened, the staff would send them home for the day. Everyone followed directions, even during such times of consequences. This was because of the trust we developed with the young people. If our participants pushed any of our boundaries, the staff would have a dialogue and hold them responsible and make necessary changes. If trust, rapport, and commitment from staff members are apparent to young people, they tend to respond more favorably.

We also wanted the youth to feel that each one had a voice. We encouraged them to express their opposition and to speak up against situations that felt were in the wrong. The key was to teach *how* to do this in a resourceful and articulate manner.

I remember one incident where we had a well-known East Los Angeles Muralist, Zender, guide the group towards painting a mural. He met with a few of the youth and developed a concept drawing of a mural. The next step was to expand on the mural concept and begin the project. Unfortunately, when he was looking for feedback, some of the group's most active members were not present. We decided to continue the project without their participation. The following week, when we were going to start the mural project, the active youth immediately asked to meet with staff to discuss the situation.

Upon meeting with us, the youth expressed their disappointment. We asked them to tell us what they felt. Leo and some of the others came up with a logical reason as to why we were not being fair about the mural project by not waiting to include them. We came to a compromise by stating that we would include them if they agreed to consistently follow through with the project.

The greatest part of this process was how involved they became after we had the meeting. They all worked together to create a well-developed aesthetically pleasing mural. We never allowed much focus to be spent on deciding who was wrong, or who was right. We wanted everyone to be responsible and to follow through with their ideas and to learn to express themselves in an articulate manner when dealing with adversity.

The Story of Basco

Juan Luna, affectionately known to us as *Basco* was a street-smart, charismatic kid who had the ability to generate an environment of humor wherever he went. Basco was a physically-fit young man with an oval face and a closely sheered head. He would often wear a baseball cap to cover his haircut because he was self-conscious of the scars he had. Basco had a metal plate on one side of his head due to a high-speed car accident that he was involved in when he was thirteen. Consequently, he served four years in the California Youth Authority for his involvement, and was released at the age of seventeen.

With his dark brown eyes he had the ability to look through people who lacked authenticity; Basco did not miss a beat. He could also be serious or extremely funny, depending on the setting. While Basco had the ability to be light and happy, he also had a dark side he had no problem revealing.

One day, Basco walked into the *Impacto* building under the encouragement of Leo and Richard. Richard was another one of the youth members who was dedicated to our program. Everyone affectionately called Richard *Ratita* or "little rat person," because he possessed a few whiskers on his small chin. He was around 5'10" with a trim build. Richard was the epitome of a cool Chicano inner-city youth. He often wore baggy, precisely creased clothing, and more often than not, dressed better than me. Richard carried himself cautiously, while at the same time, he was quick-witted with his remarks and humor. Leo and Richard grew up together and were like brothers. Richard was cautious with people he did not know and was quiet and observant with me, at first. He had a natural well-developed intuition and had the ability to see a person's true colors.

Leo took it upon himself to recruit youth into the program and was often busy keeping his buddies out of trouble. I would often see Leo outside of the building reprimanding his closest peers about their negative behavior. He did this in a direct, but respectful manner.

Basco was usually one of those youth getting a lecture from Leo or from Carlos Vasquez and Rulies, sometimes by all three. Basco's comical side helped in dissipating tension and creating a festive environment, but his argumentative side often got him into trouble. He was an inquisitive young man, always questioning, wanting to know why. Basco could also be stubborn and had to be talked to about his behavior. He also had no problem expressing how he felt towards people he liked, hugging and being affectionate to everyone. Basco always had his arm around someone, staff, friends, and of course the girls, always with a smirk on his face.

On several occasions I would take him to my house. He was amazed at how many toys my sons had, "Your sons are so lucky" he said while gazing at the array of toys and games.

One time, I gave Basco and another youth a ride home on a Friday evening. I dropped the other youth off first at the Estrada Courts Projects in East Los Angeles. I made sure to wait until he was safely in his home. He waved goodbye and walked into his house.

The lighting near the area where I parked was poor. I noticed Basco, in the front seat of my car looking nervously around in different directions. I asked if he was nervous, he nodded "yes" as he pointed towards five bald muscular young men with tattoos walking towards my vehicle. He said, "I am not nervous for me.... for you. So can we stop talking about it and get the hell out of here!" His remark was eerie, because he didn't care about himself. He was more concerned about my welfare.

I was told from other staff members and from his friends that it was common for Basco to put other's welfare first. This was a youth who was very committed to our programs. In meetings he was the one who had everyone laughing and side-track the group. He attended every meeting and workshop we had at the center, often the last one to leave.

I remember one early evening, after a hectic day at *Impacto*, we decided not to have an evening leadership session. I decided to eat at my local favorite Mexican restaurant to avoid the harsh Los Angeles traffic on the way home. As I was driving into the restaurant parking lot, I noticed there was a young man riding a small bike in circles in the semi-empty street that was adjacent to the restaurant's parking lot. In the middle of the street was Basco. I yelled out, "Hey Basco what are you doing here?"

He stopped circling his bike and with a slight smile, responded by saying, "Nothing just *kicking it.* Hey Louie, what are you still doing here?"

I told him I was hungry, and wanted to miss the nightmare rush-hour traffic. I asked him why he was not at home yet. Basco put his head down and said that he had a falling-out with his father and was asked to leave the house. His eyes began to water. I asked him if he was hungry. He nodded, with a slight smile. I patted him affectionately on his upper back and opened the door to the restaurant, gesturing with my hand for him to go in.

"Okay, Basco, it's my treat… this is one my favorite places… order whatever you want." As we waited for the food, we talked about his family and the possible reasons that had led him to be kicked out of his house. He shared with me some of the personal obstacles he was having at home. I did my best to provide suggestions and encouraging words regarding his circumstances. After the meal, he mentioned how he was going to stay at a friend's house. I gave him some money to buy the clothes and hygiene items he would need. I gave him a hug, and then he got on his modest bike and darted off to his destination. Within seconds he disappeared into the forest of colorful buildings and street noises.

Eventually he patched things up with his father, and after several weeks returned home. I didn't know his dad, but I spoke with his mother on several occasions; he had a great relationship with his mom. She was always supportive of his progress and positive behavior. He shared a story about the time when he was incarcerated without privileges and his mom went above and beyond to help him out.

While in custody, Basco was in desperate need of shoes that fit. He wore a pair of old oversized, grubby, institutional tennis shoes that were issued to him. He let his mom know about his situation, so one day she came to visit wearing a brand new pair of athletic shoes that were in *his* size. During their visit, they quickly exchanged shoes when the guards were not looking. Basco told the story that he went back into his cell with brand new comfortable athletic shoes while his mother shuffled out of that visiting room with those grubby, old, institutional over-sized tennis shoes and flip-flopped her way to the parking lot. No one noticed the jailhouse issued shoes on her feet.

The staff had encouraged everyone to participate by promising they would have the opportunity to go on an excursion. We mentioned to the youth that a trip to Canada was a strong possibility. As a result, we had over thirty active teenagers take part in the leadership training. We had another fifteen who took part in other programs and would visit periodically. The staff and I were beginning to feel as if we had truly turned the program around.

Basco took advantage of the many services that were provided in the community. One time, he even suggested I come in on the weekends so that he would have somewhere to go and activities to keep him out of trouble. Over the next six months he participated in every leadership training session we offered.

We were able to connect him to a pre-college program that helped high school students facing obstacles while in high school. The program provided students with tutors and helped to better prepare them for college. Several of our youth were involved.

Another program was a community theater class. The youth learned how to act and how to put on productions. Their acting coach was Raquel Salinas, she was a knowledgeable and creative teacher. Raquel taught them how to use acting as a form of healing, as vehicle for expressing their voice through art. They often produced plays about current issues that impacted the youth and community. The theater group performed in venues all over Los Angeles.

Basco was a natural actor. I always enjoyed seeing him and his theater group, create skits and plays. They were fearless. I found that watching them practice their acting skits was more entertaining than anything on television. All of these components of *Impacto* strengthened the leadership program.

After six months into the program, we were able to organize a trip to Canada. This was an opportunity to apply the skills our participants had learned as a form of leadership and cultural exchange with various First Nation communities (Native Americans). The

Impacto team was able to raise money and gather financial support for the trip. The team consisted of twenty-one youth and eight adult chaperones. The credit for creatively attracting the necessary funds came from the director, Christine Sanchez, Carlos Vasquez, Rulies, our board of directors, Boyle Heights Youth Opportunity Movement, and Father Greg Boyle. It was all very expensive, but everything fell into place creating a trip of a lifetime for the *Impacto Leadership Program*. I felt so proud to be a part of it.

Canada

It took us three hours to fly into Vancouver. Our adventure was about to begin when we discovered that Basco didn't have his immigration papers and was detained by Canadian Customs Officials. Months before departure, we had worked thoroughly to get him cleared for the trip. Our director Christine informed us that she was going to fly back with Basco if he was not cleared. We all waited and wondered if he was going to be able to join us on this greatly anticipated journey.

Fortunately, after quite some time, he was allowed to enter Canada. We gathered our luggage, rented four mid-size vans, and drove four hours northeast to Kamloops. Our mood was elated. We caravanned and I was driving in the lead with portable radios to communicate between the vans. The youth who were riding up front on the passenger side were allowed to use the radio for communication; they were our co-pilots.

I had been to Canada many times, but for everyone else, this was their first opportunity. For most of the youth it was also their first time on an airplane. Our relationship with those youth, once strained, was developing into a safe and trusting interaction.

One of the reasons why we drove instead of flying to our final destination, Kamloops, was because I wanted to share with the group the immense overwhelming beauty of the Coquihalla Highway. This four-hour drive goes over a stunning, scenic mountain highway in British Columbia. It is one of the most breathtaking and impressive natural areas I have ever witnessed, with misty coast cedars and fir trees. The mountains are towering and majestic, and the land reveals a myriad of colors of what appears to be untouched boundless land. It reminded me of a Hawaiian word, *mana*, which translates to *someone or something with overwhelming spiritual power.* The mountain area on the Coquihalla Highway had powerful *mana* energy, and most importantly, that power pulsated from the earth through our bodies and our minds. *Mana* is what I feel whenever I drive through these mountains.

At dusk, the beauty of the mountains was intoxicating my senses. As we drove along the highway, Basco got on the radio and said, with a heavy East Los Angeles accent, "Hey man, I have never seen the snow, eh… Can we pull over and take a break?" Hearing his voice so far away from East Los Angeles brought me back to reality.

At Basco's request, we pulled over to this large patch of snow. The area was as big as a football field. The immense mountains were all around us. The panoramic view was nothing any of us were accustomed to seeing. As soon as we pulled to the side of the road and turned off the engines, I could hear the faint sound of van doors sliding open simultaneously, as these resilient teens from East Los Angeles bolted out like school children on their way to recess. Within seconds they were rolling on the snow and throwing snowballs at everyone. I could hear the echo of laughter throughout the cold Canadian air.

After only thirty minutes, the sun was about to go down for the count. We instructed everyone to return to the vans. The *Impacto* group was halfway to its destination, and darkness was descending quickly. We continued driving on the Canadian open road. The kids did an awesome job at keeping me awake.

We arrived at Kamloops around midnight. The road to our destination was up in the hills through windy, scenic dirt roads. We were going to stay for the next few days at the home of Colleen Seymour where there were creeks, enormous trees and dirt roads leading to what seemed an endless road into the forest. Our host was waiting up for us along with my long-time friend June Jules. June was one of the organizers working for the *Kamloops First Nation Band* as a youth advocate.

Once we got to Colleen's home, on an acre and a half of Canadian countryside, we set up camp and situated the sleeping arrangements. Our host had prepared a sweat lodge in her yard. Around nine young men joined me in the sweat. Tired, but in high spirits from traveling, we approached the back part of the property where the crackling sound of wood burning could be heard and smelled. There was a large bon fire, three feet high, with bright orange-yellow colors that danced majestically into the evening air. The rocks inside had been cooking for hours before our arrival.

By the time we changed into our shorts and gathered everyone together, the rocks were red hot and the sweat leader was ready to enter.

It was the first time anyone in our group had experienced a Native American traditional sweat and everyone was excited and nervous about this new experience. A line of skinny, brown bodies in swimming trunks were lined up with towels draped over their shoulders, ready to go in. One by one, each of us silently crawled in clockwise and sat cross leg on the damp cold earth. When everyone was situated, the sweat leader began.

With respect and attentiveness, the group waited for the sweat lodge leader to start the purification ceremony, done with a welcome and an opening prayer to purify the mind, spirit, and body. The youth minds and spirits were being prepared to interact with new people and experiences. The sweat also was to assist them in letting go of their city mentality and put them into a positive mindset.

During the sweat, everyone in the group prayed and had the opportunity to express themselves, creating a bond that was much needed. We stayed in for about two hours. The young men shared eloquent and encouraging words with one another and said some prayers of thanks. The sweat was calm and smooth. Coming out of the sweat cleared my senses and allowed me to enjoy the land and people in Canada at a deeper level. After the ceremony, we left the sweat lodge with a greater awareness of self and others.

We went to sleep around 2 a.m. The women had a scheduled sweat at 5 a.m. I woke up with some of the reliable youth to help the women set up the fire. The others were left in the multi-layered realm of sleep.

The morning was fresh and crisp; the sun began revealing more exquisite scenery. The *mana* was all around us. I wanted the youth to experience the clean air, silence, and natural esthetics.

Youth Interaction

While the entire trip was memorable, Basco's participation was unforgettable. His personality was quite entertaining to us and our new friends. I recall being invited to take a day of youth activities in a Powwow arena in the town of Kamloops. The arena was impressive; it had wooden bleachers and a large grassy area, as large as a baseball field. Many youth organizations in British Columbia were there to share the day with us.

Many activities took place. Powwow drummers drummed and sang traditional songs. We danced to Powwow two-step dances, and played musical chairs. My flute students were invited to play the Andean flute on the main stage. There were guest speakers and plenty of activities to get the youth to connect and have fun. We enjoyed a great lunch of Indian tacos, thick fry bread, ground beef, cheese, shredded lettuce, and diced tomatoes. Everyone enjoyed their meal while a youth drum group sang on the stage.

During lunch I saw Basco attempting to dance with some of the mothers of the youth that lived in Kamloops. Minutes later, I was surprised to see him on the main stage with the Native youth drum group. They had stopped singing and asked Basco to sing a song.

He started hitting the drum with no sense of rhythm; and in a voice that sounded like an injured animal, attempted to sing. I heard from the people in the audience, a roar of laughter and applause.

When he stopped singing he had that familiar grin on his face. As he left the stage, I waited for him by the steps and said sarcastically yet in a serious tone, "Hey Basco, they are clapping for you because you're finally getting off stage? What the heck you doing up there?" Not bothered by my sarcasm, he smiled wide and gave me a hug. I shook my head and walked away later realizing that Bosco had captured their hearts with his natural charisma.

Later that evening, June and Coleen had organized a talent show. They provided a tasty traditional meal of salmon, beef, mashed potatoes, and vegetables. They asked the youth that were present if any of them wanted to sing a song for a prize. Basco stepped up and said, "I have a song." With all the confidence of the world behind him, he walked in front of the microphone and began to sing an oldie but goodie, "Sitting in the Park."

Again, he sang off-key. I think all the reservation dogs and cats were covering their ears in pain, I know I was. Surprisingly, people started clapping and laughing. He sang that song with no fear and with a deep happiness that was contagious. Basco did not care what people thought about him; all he knew was that he was having the time of his life.

After spending three days in Kamloops, we made our way to the Neskonlith Band, about an hour away. The Kamloops youth joined us and we arrived late that afternoon at the Neskonlith Community Center. They prepared dinner for us, and invited a hand drum group to sing traditional songs. We visited for a while and left the Community Center by 6 p.m., then traveled half an hour to Neskonlith Lake, a scenic campsite near a huge lake. Large yellow cedars and pine trees surrounded the lake and hillsides. We camped out with a lot of people from Neskonlith and some youth and adults from Kamloops. We shared an early dinner, and stories, and then went to bed.

In the morning we went canoeing, took walks, played traditional games, and ate fresh-cooked salmon; baked in an underground pit. The youth had an impromptu dance in the evening under the dense trees where they found a flat clearing that created a dance floor illuminated by a circle of headlights from our vehicles.

The next day we drove back to Colleen's house. The young women in our group had decided they wanted to cook a traditional Mexican dinner for our host. They made tasty enchiladas with rice and beans. I was kicked out of the kitchen for being in the way of their mission and distracting the ladies with my teasing and joking. You do not want to mess with Mexican women when they are focused on a task like cooking. So, I went where I was appreciated, with my friends that were singing around the campfire. I played the guitar and they sang traditional songs. My friend Roxanne Tootoosis also sang several mesmerizing Cree songs with her niece. There was a festive vibe that evening. I saw smiles and laughter on everyone's face. People were coming from everywhere to be with us.

The next morning, with little sleep from singing and visiting with our friends, we packed up and drove almost two hours to the Okanagan Reserve. The Okanagan people were happy to see us and greeted us with warmth. They had set the tables and were ready when we got there, offering a delicious meal. One of the organizers, Tiffany Wilson and her family had prepared a large pot of soup with beef and vegetables along with bannock, similar to fry bread, but sweet. We slept in a meeting hall that was the size of a high school basketball court with the boys on one side and the girls on the opposite. It took the group several hours to get everyone to settle down.

The following day we participated in group activities with the youth from the Okanagan Reserve. During the evening, more people from the community joined us in playing *stick games*, a traditional form of gambling, with songs, laughter and community involvement. Some of our youth were skillful at guessing where the stick was being placed and the game requires a lot of intuition. Richard, from our leadership group, played the game like a pro.

The next day, Tiffany Wilson's family made breakfast for us. They made pancakes with eggs and bacon, orange juice, and coffee. Our director, Christine, offered to pay for the breakfast, but they would not accept it. They were extremely kind to us.

We had to drive four hours back to Vancouver that day and rented hotel rooms for the group. Rested, we made our way to the Vancouver airport the next day. The *Impacto* youth were able to visit the city and enjoy the sights.

After the weeklong experience in Canada, it was time to return to the reality of city life. It was difficult to leave because the trip had been a huge success. The entire group from Los Angeles learned a lot and they had an unforgettable reference point of the world beyond the city limits. I also felt the *Impacto* youth had a positive influence on the other youth they met on the trip. People were impressed with how these East L.A. teenagers conducted themselves. Our flight back to Los Angeles was smooth.

Once we arrived, we were picked up by a large passenger bus. The amazing quality of teenagers is how they can create a happy environment anywhere, during any situation. Once everyone was on the bus, the bus driver played trendy hip-hop dance music with his surround-sound stereo. While stuck in traffic, all the youth, and some of the adults, began dancing, oblivious to the outside world. Even I began swaying my body, when no one was looking.

We arrived in Boyle Heights and were greeted by a crowd of familiar faces who brought with them delicious food for the hungry travelers: homemade burritos, fast food breakfast sandwiches, doughnuts, and fruit juice. There was amongst us, a feeling of elation and accomplishment. We had taken a group of dedicated Boyle Heights youth on a trip to another country where they experienced a profound cultural exchange without incident or conflict. This was tribute to our hard work and dedication. Our staff and participants shared an unforgettable experience that elevated the entire community.

During the next few months, I noticed a stronger rapport with our students, something had changed in them. They had become experienced travelers and had the opportunity to see the reality of what is possible in life. The adults were also more committed to the program. We had developed a deep admiration toward the youth we worked with and they felt it. We celebrated many youth achievements: a respectable grade in school, learning a new instrument, developing a play or anything else that was positive.

Signs to Move On

Unfortunately, four months after the trip I decided to resign after almost four years of working in the Boyle Heights community; I had seen the signs. When I worked in the probation department, the signs were clear for me then too, but I ignored them. At *Impacto*, the signs were there once again, this time I chose to pay attention.

One day, when I checked out the agency van, I got into an accident as I was turning into an alley. Twenty minutes after, I parked in front of the *Impacto* building and a car drove by and did a hit-and-run on the side of the van. It made a noticeable dent on the driver's side. Later during the late afternoon, I took the youth to the hills at Griffith Park, and a coyote crossed the road while I was driving. I had been working three jobs at the time, my wife of eight years and I decided to get a divorce, and I was feeling scattered.

I put in my resignation and was ready to move on after four years of working as a consultant, mentor, coordinator, music teacher, and curriculum developer. I felt as if my obligation was complete and it was time to move on to the next calling in life.

The youth organized a going-away gathering for me at the center. They had all this great Mexican food that was cooked in my honor. We formed a circle and they shared eloquent heartfelt words that were deeply touching. As tears rolled down from my eyes, I thanked everyone with a special comment to each one. I had grown to love them.

Even though it was difficult, I knew it was time for me to move on. While in the circle with approximately forty youth and four staff members, I felt a love from them that was earned and rooted in time and trust. I remember when I first worked with them they did not trust me or my co-workers. It reminded me that the key to developing a rapport with a community is to be patient, present and committed. Trust is earned with authenticity.

A year later, the youth program lost funding and was modified. Basco dropped out of the college transition program. He reconnected with the negative element of the neighborhood and his involvement with drugs became more progressive. One night, he went on a drug deal in a volatile housing projects area where he was approached by local gang members and was shot numerous times in the chest. He died instantly at the age of eighteen. Several of the youth that lived in the projects heard the gun shots. The original leadership group and staff were devastated by his senseless death. A former gang member with many issues to overcome, we watched Basco grow into a dynamic young man bringing a lot of joy to the lives of many people. Basco's passing was so sudden. His death was truly a great loss.

Father Greg Boyle conducted the wake and funeral services. During the funeral it was evident that he had a hard time serving the mass, even though he had buried many gang members during his priesthood. The mass was at Dolores Mission, in the heart of the Boyle Heights community. The church was full with mostly young mournful faces.

I will never forget what Fathered Greg said that night during the wake. He described Basco as a young man who "carried a truth of God." Even though Basco strayed off the path of God at times, he was still able to express love and joy in a way that was contagious. During Basco's short life, he was able to entertain us, amaze us, and share his joy and his love with everyone. There was always laughter around Basco.

CHAPTER 11 FOCUS

Countless young people will be lost to the insanity of the streets if effective programs are not maintained. It's imperative that these community-based programs are financially preserved and sustained. The harshness of poverty stricken streets only provides a life of misery for countless teens. Solid and effective youth programs alter youth violence and heal our communities. With a motivated and capable team, programs are able to resolve community conflicts, heal strained relationships between adults and youth, and move eager youth to a higher level of growth and development. The possibilities are limitless. Successful and consistent programs are necessary in all communities.

CHAPTER XII

REDIRECTION COUNSELING

LOOKING BACK ON MY career in the probation department, I remember all of the many young kids I worked with, one-on-one, but Joey was special. I met him when he was incarcerated at the Youth Guidance Center in Santa Ana, California.

He was only eleven and already in custody for petty theft and probation violation. At the time, he was the youngest minor in the entire institution. The younger wards were often treated a little differently due to their immaturity. Fortunately, Joey was smart, had a good sense of humor, and was able to adapt to the youth correctional setting.

At the Youth Guidance Center, inside each unit was a main entrance with a control desk and two probation staff members. For better supervision, another staff person usually sat with the minors while they watched television. Room checks and head counts took place every fifteen minutes. This is done to ensure every youth is accounted for and to minimize potential physical altercations and escapes. If a youth was not in the day area, then he would be in his single or a two-dorm room. A minor's behavior determined which room he was given. Joey was usually in a single room.

One of Joey's challenges at the Center was his inability to sit still. He was often in trouble for creating problems with his excessive playful nature. I enjoyed spending time with him. He was a funny kid and had an innocent child-like energy. It seemed as if he did not have a care in the world; all he cared about was being a kid.

Regardless of Joey's playful endeavors, I was able to develop a rapport with him. He would often talk to me about his favorite cartoons and loved quoting youthful action movies. Most of the time, all he wanted to do was play, finding amusement in the mundane things. In a way, I admired his innocence. It was a quality that was rare in an institutional setting. Most young men and women lose this quality when they get caught up in the system. It was refreshing to see this little guy, full of life and energy, not being affected by his environment.

Sometimes, during my break, I would visit his unit. The minute he saw me, Joey would raise his hand to get permission to speak with me. Most of the time, he walked briskly towards me, ignoring instructions from the staff to sit down and not run in the unit. The probation staff often gave Joey a break, due to his age. His youthful spontaneity did not coincide with the structured institutional environment.

It was this same energy that everyone appreciated, that got Joey into trouble. Some of his consequences were: loss of free-time activities, early bed times, and time-outs in his room. These consequences were difficult because of Joey's impatience. I would often listen to his complaints about the personalities and the strict rules of staff in his unit. I constantly tried to advise him the best I could. Every so often he would take my advice, but most of the time, he wouldn't.

He reminded me of my nephews, his age. Since he was so young I believed that he had a chance of eventually living a healthy lifestyle. I had a lot of faith in him; all he needed was the proper guidance and he could make it. After four months, he was released to his mother. I said goodbye to him, hoping the experience taught him to make better choices with his life. I wanted him to have a clean slate.

About five years later, I accepted an over-time shift at the main Juvenile Hall in the City of Orange. I was escorting a group of minors from their court hearing back to the facility, adjacent to the courthouse. It was a routine line movement with the minors walking in controlled line movements from one location to another without talking and their hands behind their backs. As I entered Juvenile Hall, out of the corner of my eye I saw three youth sitting on the booking area bench and heard a young man say in a deep voice, "Hey! Mr. Ruan, I am back!" When I turned, I looked at a hardened, muscular, bald-headed gangster; it was Joey. He spoke in short and to-the-point sentences. He was going through the booking process with two other rough-looking kids.

Joey was glad to see me, but he had changed. Instead of the young kid who liked cartoons and movies, I saw a young man who appeared to carry a lot of anger. When he saw me, he refrained from enthusiastically running or walking towards me. Instead he acted restrained, with a tough street bravado. I could tell that Joey had grown into one of those youth who had learned how to control and manipulate his environment. In the manner the other youth responded to him, he had established himself as a leader.

From that day forward, I noticed that Joey was nothing like the kid he used to be. He became difficult to deal with in the institution. Joey was skilled at intimidating the new probation staff as well as his peers. He still maintained a familiar respect towards me, he needed assistance probation was not able to provide. After all, probation staff was not equipped to deal with Joey's core issues or provide him with the necessary resources to guide him in the right direction.

Joey was eventually released after serving six months. He returned to a harsh gang and drug-infested neighborhood with absent parents and no resources for young Latino men. He was embraced by the destructive side of life that welcomed him with open arms. I never saw Joey again, but I would hear rumors of his street exploits from the other youth that knew him. As my career moved along in the Probation Department, I experienced working with several youth with similar beginnings as Joey; they spent their young years in and out of institutions, and eventually graduated to the adult prison system.

Working with troubled youth like Joey can be complex. As a sixteen year old, he was angry, intimidating, and had no fear. Most people walk away from young men like him. For many, it is easier to give up and say, "Just lock them all up." And while that mentality has been the most prevalent approach, what happens when we set them free?

◎ ◎ ◎

Resilient Persistence

I like what author, Luis Rodriguez tells his audiences: "If you want to be tough on crime, work with the gang kids on the street." That statement says it all: It is not easy to change these kids, but it is worth it? That is what being *tough on crime* should mean. The prevalent solution is to be tough by putting them away and not dealing with the core issues. Locking up a human being for a prolonged period of time causes them to become institutionalized, get angrier, develop mental health issues, become more criminally sophisticated, and become a heavier burden on the taxpayer and society. According to various statistics, the cost of one year of incarceration per prisoner is approximately $50,000 per year in California, not including medical care.

Many of the men that I have worked with, who were incarcerated for prolonged periods of time, felt more comfortable being behind bars than on the outside; they had become institutionalized. It only makes sense to try and help kids change their paths when they are still young and prevent this from happening. But for too many parents, teachers, and social workers, it is easier to give up.

Working with troubled youth is not easy. It takes time and patience to go beyond the protective shell of a young person who has been through the system. People who are most effective with at-risk kids are the ones who possess this understanding.

Mother's Approach to Listening Skills

My mother had an interesting natural approach with her down-to-earth counseling skills when assisting friends of the family. Often, relatives visited my parent's home for the purpose of seeking out advice from my mother with their problems. For me, it was annoying to see people in our home crying and spending valuable time with my mom.

The effective part of her counseling was that she was an excellent listener. She listened with her heart and mind to understand where the person was coming from. My siblings and I understood that Mom needed her space with these individuals. My mom had a routine that worked for her. In my later years when it was time for me to develop my counseling techniques, I had a deeper appreciation of her abilities.

Her first step was to make the person in need feel comfortable and relaxed, as they sat in the warmth of our kitchen table. My mom would serve them a cup of steaming herbal tea or coffee with Mexican sweetbread. At times, if they were hungry they ate a delicious Mexican meal. Once settled, they began communicating the causes of their problem. During the conversation my mom interjected words, phrases, or stories to get them to get to the heart of the problem. She was an attentive listener and waited patiently until they were finished explaining their situation.

Once the person was finished talking, my mother would then ask questions in a non-threatening manner. She did this to smoothly guide the person to reflect on his or her behavior. Eventually they would express deep heartfelt emotions, becoming tearful, communicating feelings of remorse. When the individual was finished talking, she tactfully and with timing provided words of encouragement and suggestions. They always left the house with their head up and with a better attitude. This scenario was a common occurrence at my house.

My mother taught me that listening is an art. These visitors had real life problems that needed immediate attention. The majority of them could not afford the luxury of paying for therapy, but my mother was there with her attentive listening skills and her *yerba buena* tea.

Listening is a simple powerful method of healing.

Rapport

I remember when I first started working in the probation department, with a middle-aged Chicano probation officer named Jose Rodriguez. Jose and I patrolled the neighborhood streets where most of the youth and adults of his caseload lived.

We were in a conspicuous county probation vehicle when he pulled the car into a driveway where three gang members were standing. He rushed out of the vehicle toward a gang member and demanded to see his inner forearms. The slender gang member put his arm out nonchalantly, like doing it was routine for him. Jose looked at his fresh needle marks and asked him, "Why are you using?" He then gave the gang member a very light, fatherly tap on the face with the palm of his hand. I quickly grabbed the radio and was about to call for back up.

Nursing his cheek the gang member responded like a son would to a father, "Hey Jose, why did you do that for?"

Jose responded, "Next time I am going to arrest you. You better stay clean or you are going back to jail."

The only reason Jose was able to get away with that is because he had a solid rapport with the young man. I am not saying to do exactly what he did. If somebody else would have tried the same approach, it could have been an explosive situation. What is important in becoming effective is to develop a positive rapport. Jose always had a well-developed interaction with the young men on his caseload this was created by him working many years in the community he served. Everyone knew him, or of him. Jose was respected and well-known for his tough but compassionate approach towards the neighborhood youth and adult probationers.

How to Connect

1. Be your word

The best way to develop credibility is by being consistent with your word. In the Mexican culture, it is called *Palabra*, which translates to being a person of integrity and being true to your word. This concept comes from the great Toltecs from Old Mexico.

Keeping your word with everyone in your circle enhances relationships and trust. This is something that our society has minimized. This ancient teaching should be applied to all relationships. People will know if a person follows through with what they say. News spreads like wildfire in the community when an individual goes back on their word, or when an individual follows through.

2. Keep Promises

Youth have experienced a lot of inconsistencies from adults in their environment. Do not make any promises you cannot keep. In this society, there are many examples of leaders and role models who do not keep their word. If everybody kept their word, things would be much more pleasant.

3. Accountability

Young people will be quick to point out your inability to maintain your word. You can also use this in your favor. If you are keeping your word, make them keep their word, as well. Follow-through keeps everybody accountable. It is something we can model through our everyday actions.

4. Respect

Do not embarrass or humiliate youth in front of their peers. Treat them with dignity and respect, no matter who they are or what they have done in the past. When I worked with gang members I never tried to humiliate them in front of their peers. If pushed into a corner they will retaliate with verbal threats or sometimes violence. There are better ways to deal with these situations. One way is to call them to the side, away from their audience, and confront them one-on-one...*Respect applies to all human beings.*

5. *Understanding*

Make an effort to understand the youth you are working with. Learn about their culture, language, hobbies, music, friends, neighborhoods, and family structure. In the Latino community, when an individual that is from a different culture makes an effort to learn the culture and the language in a humble manner, it creates a solid connection with that particular group. Such knowledge will bring you closer to their world by creating a better understanding of what they go through. Remember, lofty attitudes only create polarization... *Nobody is better than anybody else.*

6. *Commitment*

Maintain your commitment through your actions. For example, it's time for you to go home and a youth wants to speak with you and your response is, "I cannot talk to you because it is after 5 p.m., and I am off the clock." You just showed them a lack of commitment... *Make the time!*

7. *Authenticity*

Youth will see right through you if you are not sincere or if you are trying to be something you are not. I have seen educated men get tattoos on their bodies with the intent to impress and get some kind of camaraderie with the youth.

Or they might start dressing like gang members when it's not part of their upbringing. It has nothing to do with ethnic background. Kids want somebody that is real, has a compassionate heart and is able to keep their word... *Just be yourself.*

8. *Honesty*

Youth will trust you more if you are always truthful. Make it a habit to be upfront and clear with your communication. They will be grateful for your honesty.

It's Not Personal

At another point in my career, I worked with high-risk youth for a year in a program called *Rites of Passage* in the middle of the Nevada desert. Young men were from all over California and Nevada were sent there as a last resort. In the early days, some of the youth were well-known for throwing rattlesnakes at staff they did not like, or breaking staff with institutional mind games. On my first day, I was tested in many ways by both the staff and the inmates. The staff did not know if they could trust me because I was new, and the inmates did not like me just because I was there.

As I was strolling down the walkway between one of the quantum dorms (long military dwellings that hold numerous beds) and the kitchen, one young man said in a harsh manner, "New booty... hey man... nice ass."

I responded in a serious, professional tone. The inmate just walked away. From that point on, he never attempted to challenge me again.

Some staff reactions to remarks like that can be exaggerated. They would *cuss* out the inmate or give him extensive consequences. The youth now knows what bugs the staff and will try to do it again and again. I have observed youth studying the adults and looking for weaknesses. As a person working with at-risk youth, I needed to be several steps ahead. Often, their hostility will be directed at me, but I understood I wasn't the cause of it. I was there to help them redirect.

If You Help One, You Help Many

I have had seasoned adult gang members tell me, "You will never get rid of gangs… they are too strong. They control a lot of what happens on the street." I have had co-workers; professional highly-educated people tell me that my years of working with youth were a waste, "They are just too screwed-up, Louie!"

I think about such words, and it saddens me to think people have become so apathetic toward our youth. My response is simple, "If I help one, I help many." If I focus all my energy on one-troubled teenager, I assist them in becoming a healthy and empowered individual. They in turn, may have a family and kids one day, and if they are not healed or lead to a healthier path, their pain and dysfunction will affect their entire community and their children will perpetuate the same. This is powerful. I have seen this. These former gang members that have healed will duplicate the same work, maybe better. Their influence is possibly much more effective and at deeper levels than someone with multiple degrees. It is important to be open to creative ways of reaching our youth.

Walk your Talk

I was asked by a friend to talk to two teenage boys who were having behavioral problems at school and at home. According to their parents, they were ditching school and experimenting with drugs and alcohol. Their behavior was out-of-control. They did not listen or respect their parents. These kids had complete control of the house. When the parents asked their kids to complete their chores and to do homework, the kids laughed and ignored them.

I met with the parents first and explained what I was going to do. Then, I asked the two boys if I could talk to them in private. They let me into their shared bedroom. It had two single beds opposite of each other, a small television, and wall-to-wall posters of young females in scanty bikinis. I asked them, "Are your parents okay with all this?" pointing to the posters. They snickered at my modesty.

"Yeah, they don't care. They are too busy doing their drugs," the younger one said in a blunt tone as he threw a baseball up in the air while lying on the bed. I had known both boys and their parents for a long time and was considered close to the family. I had an automatic rapport with them and a trust was already established between us. I also had leverage because I was older. I continued with a series of questions about their situation. They were fairly open and honest.

I asked the two teenage boys and their parents if I could speak with all of them together; they all agreed. We sat in the living room and I lectured the entire family about the importance of parental responsibility. The reason the kids were having so many problems was because the parents were abusing drugs in front of them. The parents were being inconsistent with their expectations. The teenagers were decent kids. In any stable environment, they would have excelled, but kids learn from their environment.

It is important to practice the philosophy that we preach. If we practice it, we become a powerful teacher and a positive example. What we do with the youth will become rooted. Unfortunately, as the two brothers got older they were in and out of adult institutions for dealing drugs, something their own parents taught them to do.

Look at People's Hearts

One element of the Navajo people I respected was how they were able to look at the person's heart and not their ethnic background. I participated in ceremonies with the Navajo people. The few non-Navajos who were invited were accepted and sometimes adopted because they possessed a compassionate humble heart and the right attitude of being open and accepting.

Racial division separates us and hinders progress. We need to look at the hearts of our youth and not how they look. We cannot work with people if we focus on their appearance. I have worked with young men and young women who were gay, gang members with frightening tattoos that covered their entire faces, youth with piercings all over their bodies, gothic youth, punk rockers with creative hairstyles, and many other young people in various subcultures. How they looked never mattered to me, what mattered most was their hearts and how they were as a human being. If we are not able to see beyond the façade, then we get stuck.

Balanced Approach

One big mistake I used to make when working with youth was to be so enthusiastic to help them that I would inadvertently do everything for them. It is okay to be generous and helpful, but only to a certain point. Remember, there is a fine line between helping someone with their development and impeding their growth.

There was a time in my life when I would work to create job opportunities for my clients, drive them around town for errands and job interviews, and even lend them money. I soon learned that by over-extending myself I accomplished less than if I had taught them how to become more resourceful. Being too available made me open to manipulation and perpetuated dependency. I wanted to be more effective.

This reminds me of my first excursion and what I had learned. In the *Beyond Limits Program*, we had provided everything for the youth at first and discovered we had too many behavioral problems. When we asked our participants to assist us in raising the money, there was more appreciation and commitment to the outcome. To run an efficient and effective program, we learned to create a balanced approach and allow consideration for special needs.

I recall an eighteen year old gang member I had known for a few years, Manny. He asked me if he could borrow money because several of the neighborhood youth were going to physically harm him if he did not pay off a debt. Manny pleaded with me and indicated he would do what it took to repay me. I gave him $30 and said, "I am going to pick you up tomorrow." Manny nodded in relief and was content to receive the money.

Early the next morning, I went and got him out of his comfortable bed and drove him to my house. Once we arrived, I asked him if he was ready to work. He looked confused and said, "I thought you were taking me hiking or something?"

"Not this time. Grab all my window screens and take them outside and wash them thoroughly. When you are finished, clean all the windows."

"For what?"

"Do you actually think I am a rich man? We are not here to relax or to *kick it*. You are going to wash all of the screens and windows in my house and when you're finished I have more work for you. Nothing in life is free, *Homey*!"

Manny smiled with a surprised look and said, "*Dang.*"

He did an excellent job on my screens and even my wife was impressed. It is important to teach young men that things do not come easy for any of us. If you allow people to take advantage of your generosity, they will continue and continue. My job was to teach him values, not to make his life easier, or to be his buddy.

◎ ◎ ◎

Be Realistic

When I first began my work in institutions, I stood next to an inmate who was waiting to go to court. I could feel a lot of anger and negativity from him. He did not have to say anything; his energy said it all; it was overwhelming. It was as if a dark negative cloud surrounded his spirit. Not knowing his background, I stepped away from him, noticing that other youth were doing the same. Later that day, I discovered he had been incarcerated for raping several pregnant women. I do not know if a hundred years of therapy could help that particular young man, and there are cases where some people are just too dangerous, too damaged.

This is something to consider... some youth are way out there and need a lot more help than any one person can provide. Often, you may be faced with a judgment call on who you can help and who you cannot. It is important to remember, we all have our limits.

◎ ◎ ◎

Sometimes You Need to Step Back

You may face a situation when your client may not be ready to be helped. Perhaps you have tried everything to help your client wake-up, but he or she rejects all of your efforts. You may be frustrated, lost all your patience, throwing your hands up in frustration. Whenever I would get to that point, I would say, "I care for you, and I wish the best for you... I know you can do it, but for some reason you are not ready."

219

You will always have other clients who are more serious and enthusiastic about improving their lives. There are also some youth who will never be ready. If people are not motivated to help themselves after resources have been put in place, they are not ready. We cannot make people understand that they possess the key to their own healing. That is something they have to discover on their own. Pray for them and have faith in your prayers. When they are ready, they will come back.

Setting Boundaries

Years ago I was assigned to work in an all-teenage female unit. I was conducting a group counseling session with ten juvenile female inmates. During the middle of my session, one them interrupted and crudely asked, "Mr. Ruan, how is your sex life... got any lately?" The other girls giggled and waited for my response.

I looked at the young woman and in a firm tone stated, "Young lady that is inappropriate... you need to go to your room and think about what you said... and I will be expecting an apology before I go home." Embarrassed, she left the room.

This happened within a matter of seconds. She eventually apologized before I finished my shift, and I never had that problem again with her or any of the other female inmates. If I would have not addressed her remark, I would have lost credibility with these youth. The manner in which a person deals with specific behaviors will determine the way inmates/people will treat them in the future.

Another time, I remember hearing a story about an inmate who was masturbating in front of a female staff member when she was doing a room check; he timed it perfectly to masturbate when she looked into his room. She just crossed her arms, looked at him, and said sarcastically, "You better put that thing away, if you value your future." The young man was embarrassed and caught off guard. He was expecting to shock her, but it backfired on him. She followed up with confronting his behavior and issuing him a fair consequence. Needless to say, he never did it again.

There were other times when I would invite a kid in one of my programs to have dinner at my home. Once in my vehicle, I would tell them *up-front* that the only person who changes the radio station in my car is me. There is certain music that I do not need to hear. I would also let them know that in my house there would not be any gang-related behavior or foul language and that they were expected to be respectful towards my family. They never tried to test these boundaries.

Maintain clear and consistent boundaries when dealing with youth, if not, they will test limits. Understand that many of them never had rules or boundaries in their environment. Setting boundaries is what makes your job easier and protects you. They are not only necessary, but crucial to be effective.

Putting Success in the Proper Perspective

It was over fifteen years ago when I observed a young man named Wayne. He was difficult; he did not care about anything and had no fear of anyone. He was always fighting with his peers and challenging staff. On his first day in our facility, I watched this tall and very skinny kid telling off a staff member twice his size, calling out an array of verbal threats. My first impression of Wayne was that he needed a lot of guidance and counseling; I felt compassion for his situation. Even though he had an enormous amount of anger, you could see that he was hurting and needed help. I was up to the challenge when my co-worker said to me, "Meet Wayne. He is on your caseload."

Unfortunately, I only had him for one day. Wayne was unexpectedly transferred to a location that was more secure with intense supervision. He returned after thirty days with a better attitude. Sometimes, when young men are kept away from their peers and are allowed to return, they come back with a more positive attitude.

Wayne had been sentenced to serve one year. After returning, he began working on improving his situation. He became one of the group leaders, a community council member, and eventually his positive behavior helped him to receive more privileges and outside activities. He was intelligent, loved to read books, and started learning new things. After his release, we kept in contact.

He called me six months after his release from his grandmother's house, sounding a bit depressed. I asked him what was going on. He said he felt like a failure. I asked him to be more specific. Wayne stated that he was nineteen and still had not graduated from high school.

I said, "Wait a minute. Have you been arrested since your release when I was your counselor?"

"No."

"Have you used drugs?"

"No"

"Are you still on probation?"

He answered, exasperated, "No!"

"Then you are a success! Most of the guys you were in custody with are either dead or in prison. Most of those guys you were doing time with are still doing time. So you, my friend, are a success."

Often people look for major events as marks of success such as graduating from college, or working in a high paying job. Success is something that might seem easy to achieve by one person, but difficult to another person. I find that it is best to pay attention to even the smallest milestones and to try and focus on the progress and not perfection.

Self Evaluation

It is helpful to evaluate the approach you take during complicated situations. For example, I evaluate how I deal with situations that become volatile and pose a threat. I ask myself how I can obtain better results if the situation recurs. *What would I change about how I handled that? What could I do to prevent it from happening again?*

Taking a step back and reflecting has helped me to look at the way I do things in order to improve my performance, the next time. As we all know, history has a way of repeating itself. It is in the form of rigorous self-evaluation that we can avoid making careless decisions that might create more problems.

I have come across many youth like Joey who were raised inside the system. Most of who remain incarcerated in the countless prisons of the California Department of Corrections. There has to be another alternative to the inevitable progression to prison. The approach with high-risk youth is not always simple, but with some of these tools and with an abundance of patience, we will be able to produce improved results. To guide our troubled youth towards a *Journey to the Mountain Within* requires implementation and the consistency of action.

CHAPTER 12 FOCUS

High-risk youth are easily lost in the Juvenile Justice System. If ignored, they will become criminally sophisticated adults. These adults will become a severe financial strain and a hazard to society. That is why it is imperative to work together during the early stages of their criminal involvement. To redirect this way of life, it is necessary to have a basic knowledge of environmental issues, and interact with a sense of respect and accountability. Be consistent with your actions and promises. Understand that healing takes time; you are a guide, a mirror, and a reminder of what is achievable. Ultimately, the client has to decide what direction to take. They will heal on their time, not yours. With a compassionate approach we will instill hope and the option of a better life.

CHAPTER XIII

HOW TO REACH HIGH RISK YOUTH

I TOOK MY LOVE FOR martial arts with me from childhood to adulthood and during my early years in the probation department I signed up for a self-defense training class. The training was in Aikido, a non-violent form of Japanese martial arts that utilizes circular wristlocks to redirect physical aggression. It redirects physical aggression through blending and through movement of energy. For many of the probation employees, learning how to protect yourself is important because physical altercations are frequent inside juvenile institutions. Sometimes there were riots, fights, and assaults against staff.

On one occasion, several minors attacked a male co-worker who was working the night shift. When he was not looking, they slammed a metal stool into his back. His body hit the floor; they then grabbed his keys and escaped. Unfortunately, the staff member suffered permanent back injuries.

I enjoyed my job, but I was not going to allow that to happen to me. My intention was to do everything to prevent any potential physical aggression that could cause harm to me or one of the wards. Most of the young men in custody were comfortable dealing with their emotions through physical assaults. They spent most of their day doing push-ups and lifting weights. Many of these kids did not look like teenagers, they resembled grown men. Several of them could bench-press over 300 hundred pounds.

Because of these factors, I needed specialized skills for protection just in case a possible physical altercation presented itself. I did not want to resort to using karate to defend myself, because it has the ability to cause great bodily damage. Karate uses punches, chops and kicks to attack the vulnerable areas of the body. I understood the value of using the skill, but the reality was that I was working with at-risk teenagers. My goal was to never walk into the situation using a skill that could harm them. I also knew I needed to learn another method that would not cause serious physical damage to them or me. I just wanted to learn how to restrain them temporarily until they were able to gain control of themselves without anyone getting hurt.

Aikido for Juvenile Correctional Institutions
The probation training coordinators annually assigned probation staff and personnel to a self-defense training class geared towards institutional conflicts. The training was held in one of the vacant county training rooms. A group of fifteen of my coworkers was ready to learn from our instructor. Since the instructor was running a few minutes late, I had the chance to visit with friends and

coworkers that were assigned to different institutions and field offices. Suddenly, a small, thin, elderly Asian man strolled into the probation training room. One of our administrators introduced him: "This is Mr. Wong... he will be teaching you techniques that you will find useful in your work."

Even though I had studied martial arts in my youth, I still had a difficult time accepting that an elderly Asian man was going to teach us to defend ourselves in dangerous situations; after all, he was older than all of us trainees. Needless to say, over the next two days, he quickly altered my attitude regarding his abilities.

Mr. Wong had a great sense of humor and was a knowledge-able teacher who was capable of escaping from any possible physical scenario. He was patient and strong for a man his age, even when I tried to test his abilities. He was able to skillfully redi-rect all my attacks with his effective Aikido techniques.

Since I was one of the main jokers in the class, I was periodi-cally volunteered to be the attacker during his demonstrations. The moves he taught were aesthetically beautiful with what seemed to be effortless circular Aikido moves that frequently sent my body soaring across the room. I was impressed with this type of non-vio-lent martial arts. Not designed to be offensive, Aikido is a blend-ing of energy and redirection of linear attacks. The energy and intensity of an attack is used to manipulate, control, and redirect energy. Aikido techniques are neither overpowering nor retalia-tory, but are rather meant to neutralize the attack.

I learned about re-directing energy, remaining balanced and having a relaxed mind. The instructor stressed how to use the weight and force an attack to create harmony. We were taught to never use strength against strength. The techniques he taught us were simple, but ingenious. I had never seen anything that possessed the cleverness and efficiency of Aikido. I continued to go through my yearly training in self-defense with Mr. Wong.

Years later, I took a semester of Aikido at California State University in Long Beach with Mr. Rod Kobayashi. An older Japanese gentleman with contagious laughter, he was a dedicated and highly developed *Sensei* of Aikido. It was obvious that he loved to teach. He focused a lot on breathing and the *Ki* energy.

He taught that the *Hara,* located about two inches below the navel, is the body's source of *Ki* energy. One of the main principles of Aikido is to extend your *Ki* from your *Hara.* If an individual focuses his or her energy in the power center of the stomach, it makes one strong, focused, and balanced. I have witnessed demonstrations where numerous students could not push someone who is focusing on the *Hara* in their stomach. Once, I saw five guys attempt to push and drag the instructor focused on his *Ki* energy, and could not do it. A skilled Aikido practitioner will focus on his breathing while utilizing his *Ki* energy. It is a relaxed, smooth, attentive state. A master in Aikido could toss multiple attackers like rag dolls using the concept of *Ki.*

It is similar when negative energy is aimed at a person. Negative energy, such as hurtful personal remarks or negative manipulation, is energy that can be redirected with the philosophy of Aikido. The way I see the *Ki* energy working, is for people to remain balanced and not to react with their ego. If we stay balanced and focused on our purpose, we can facilitate our job much better and redirect negative remarks. By not redirecting our focus we can become bitter, angry, frustrated, or vindictive.

Flexibility

In any martial arts, flexibility is the foundation and much time and effort is placed on becoming flexible. It prevents injuries and enhances the body's ability to execute complicated techniques and to be able to control the degree of power of each strike. In working with at-risk youth, there are many situations that do not always go as planned and unexpected events. We must be able to bounce back like a ball. Flexibility is a vital quality to possess, and it prevents frustration and disappointment.

This reminds of me of a time when I was hiking up a mountain top in Southern California during the mid-nineties. The location I was hiking was over 7,000 feet in elevation. At this height, granite and dry shrubs dominated the terrain. Once I arrived at the top, I could feel the strong wind. On the side of the mountain I saw a delicate colorful flower growing in an area that was difficult for anything to grow. I stopped and rested on a rock and gazed at it for a while. I was surprised at how something so beautiful could grow in a cold and windy harsh environment.

The flower on the side of the mountain appeared to be fragile, but it was resilient and swayed with the direction of the wind. It did not fight nature and instead moved with the force of the wind. The same principle applies to environments where we work with at-risk youth. Sometimes things do not go as planned; many times we do not have the money or resources to do what we know would be best. It is important to find a healthy way to be flexible and to *just go with the flow* in regard to the resources we have or situation we find ourselves in.

Balance

A Samurai warrior was calmly enjoying a meal at a restaurant in old Japan when a slightly inebriated man approached his table and challenged him to a duel. The Samurai continued to eat his meal while the man persisted in an attempt to provoke him with personal insults. Again, the Samurai focused on his meal, ignoring the agitator. He tried everything to provoke the focused Samurai, and out of frustration, the obnoxious drunkard spit on his face.

Within seconds, the Samurai drew his sword and assumed the position to strike. Realizing what he was about to do, the Samurai hesitated, replaced his sword, and briskly walked away. He did not want to respond to the man with anger as there was no honor in it. He could have easily hurt the challenger, but refused, under those circumstances.

That story has always reminded me of a time when I was working with *Rites of Passage*, a youth program facility in the Nevada Desert. On my first day, I was giving directions for a young man to clean his room. In a matter of seconds, he began arguing with me and then spit in my face. He responded with a barrage of racial slurs: "I ain't listening to you... damn beaner! Come on Motherfucker... I'll send you back to Mexico!"

I can still remember how the blood rushed to the back of my neck over his words. Instead of getting angry or calling him names I remained calm. I unconsciously applied the idea of redirecting energy. Since his behavior was so disruptive, we escorted him to the section of the camp for the youth that could not be with the general population. The young man was given appropriate consequences for his behavior. Since I was new in that facility and was the only Chicano counselor, he was testing me. After some time, he began to open up to me and I never had a problem with him again.

If that situation had happened at a different time, perhaps my response would not have been as favorable. The point is that it is important to stay balanced and not allow the negative ego to dominate decisions. We must make an effort to deal with situations with attentiveness, clarity, and balance. Many of these youth have anger that has been there for a long time. I know his anger toward me was based on stress and unresolved issues and I was just the target at the time; it really was not personal.

Be aware that the balanced state does not come naturally. It is easy to allow the ego to be lured into a state of imbalance. Once we are out of balance, we are open and vulnerable to our negative ego. When he spit on me, a part of me wanted to throw him out the window, but fortunately, I was able to remain calm and deal with his hostility. It takes effort to be balanced.

At a different level, try not to allow resentment to grow between your co-workers, family, and your clients as you try to do this.

Voice your resentments and/or concerns to a spouse, a friend, or someone who will listen. Write it down or talk to the person involved if you must.

I have noticed that when I express my truth to someone with whom I have resentment, it clears the air between us. Sometimes it takes several conversations in order to do this, but it is worth it. The mind must be clear in order to be in a balanced state and to be effective when working with people.

Protective Understanding

In any form of martial arts it is crucial to have a protective guard, a stance, how hands are positioned to avoid serious injuries from an unexpected attack. This manner of thinking can be applied to working with people and being able to understand an individual's unpredictability that is rooted in their past. In my case, one of the first lessons I wished I could have learned earlier in my career was to possess a protective understanding when working with at-risk youth. It would have saved me from a lot of disappointment.

During my early years working in the probation department, a young man named Paco, asked me to help him. He was only seventeen, deeply involved in gang life, and wanted out. I enthusiastically agreed to help and enrolled him in a substance abuse program, individual counseling, group counseling, parent counseling sessions, my gang redirection program, and gave him numerous books to read about his cultural history and self-growth. I spent hours talking with him, listening to his problems, and giving him advice. We planned a strategy to keep him out of trouble upon release.

After serving six months, on his release date, I was proud of all the work we had accomplished. I believed he was going to make it; he was fully engaged in his healing. He was a hard worker, intelligent, and made a commitment to change his life. Paco agreed to take part in the *Beyond Limits Program* and was scheduled to participate in my first hiking excursion to Mt. Whitney.

Two days before the backpacking excursion, I received a collect call from county jail. "Mr. Ruan, I am really sorry. I am *busted* again and can't go on the trip," he said, disappointed and ashamed. Six months later he was sentenced for a prolonged period of time in state prison for grand theft auto. Due to my naiveté, I took it personally when I heard the news. I immediately felt as if I had failed him. I went home after work and felt a deep sadness. In our training in the probation department, they tell us not to take these incidents personally, but even that warning could not prevent my disappointment.

I remembered feeling as if I did something wrong. I believed that maybe if I had been tougher on him, maybe if I would have worked more on family issues, maybe if I would have gotten him a job, or maybe, if I had been more demanding on his parents, he would have done better on the outside. Over time, I realized that my compassion for these kids only grew stronger and stronger, and while I tried to help as many as possible, I could not reach everyone. To save every kid with a problem was not something that could be done in my lifetime. I needed to understand that they had a say and a choice in their lives, and decisions.

When working with either youth or adults, I had to learn that an hour, three months, or six months of time in a facility cannot change anything they have experienced prior to getting incarcerated. Transformation is difficult, but not impossible. Many of these youth have undergone years of negative conditioning and trauma.

One session will not undo everything, no matter how smart or experienced you are. It has taken sometimes two to six years to get youth out of the gang lifestyle. I know gang members and drug addicts who have healed themselves late in life, in their thirties or forties, before they decided to make drastic changes in their lives. It is a gradual process. It depends on how much effort the individual is willing to put in and the individual's attitude. Like the martial artist, the individual must be willing to work hard to transform and develop, otherwise the practice is useless.

Let the Crisis Come In

In Mandarin, the word *crisis* translates into two meanings: danger and opportunity. For martial artists, the energy from an attack is inevitable. The importance is placed on what the individual does with that force. People can get hurt in a crisis or they can be guided to a positive direction of healthy learning. Do not be afraid of a crisis. If it feels as if a crisis is coming, you must allow it to happen. It could be the catalyst that an individual needs.

If the behavior or the lifestyle of the person you are working with was caused or was affected by a crisis such as divorce, separation, incarceration, or loss of a loved one, it is also an opportunity to initiate self-evaluation. This is always productive because it creates growth and healing. It brings out the negative behavior and forces the person to create an alternative that will not bring forth discomfort. Like boiling water, liquid will only transform to vapor with steady or intense heat. Sometimes people need a lot of heat to transform.

I once took an eighteen year old gang member, Raymond, on a hiking excursion in the Arizona Mountains. At the time, he was abusing drugs and alcohol and had a destructive attitude. Raymond was consistently thoughtless with people around him. He was selfish, only cared about his gang friends, getting high, and what he could get away with in life. His parents were decent, hardworking people who did not know what to do about their son's behavior.

They wanted him to be part of an excursion I organized in the Coconino National Forest in Northern Arizona. My close friend Jerome Towne assisted in coordinating the trip. Jerome, a Diné man with many years of experience working with youth, was a drug and alcohol counselor. Jerome was thin and of medium height, and his knowledge of Diné culture, made him excellent at connecting with the young people. We took mostly kids from the Navajo Land on this trip.

During the camping trip, Raymond did not participate in the scheduled activities. He would go out of his way to disrupt the positive activities we were trying to create. It got to the point where the adults and youth were fed up with his behavior. I noticed that the other youth began confronting him in Navajo. I did not understand, but I could tell what they were saying. His passive-aggressive behavior was disrupting the cohesiveness of the group.

After numerous counseling sessions, Raymond admitted he was an alcoholic and was experimenting with serious drugs. After learning this, I knew a confrontation was necessary. I would have to shake things up and get to the core of the problem. Jerome and I were waiting for him to own up to his behavior. Once he took that step, we were able to help him, and he was able to help himself.

Jerome and I gave him guidance and offered to get him involved with a treatment program and counseling. He said he was not interested. After the *outing*, while driving the youth back to their homes, I called Raymond's parents from a gasoline station and explained what he had been doing and described his present attitude. We arranged for the parents to drive to the home of one of the staff and meet us for a family intervention. I did not tell Raymond because he would have found a way to get out of it. He told me that if I called his parents, he would disappear. I felt this was the perfect opportunity to address his drug and alcohol problem.

His parents met us at my friend's house. When he saw his parents enter the house, Raymond wanted to run, but I stood in the way of the door and his brother blocked him. I told Raymond to sit down. After Jerome and I spoke with Raymond's parents regarding his behavior on the trip, his mother became tearful. For the first time he admitted to his parents that he needed help, and that he was going through a difficult time with drugs and alcohol.

Raymond agreed to accept help from his family and to accept help from others. That was the first and most important step for

Raymond and his family. Three years later, he was able to change his life with the support of family and traditional Navajo forms of healing. His extreme behavior during the outing was a necessary crisis that opened the door to dialogue and healing.

Have a Sense of Humor

I believe humor is the best medicine in many situations. When I was working at the Youth Center in Santa Ana, I utilized an unorthodox approach that proved to be successful. The supervisor of the girls unit had asked me to speak with Maria, a young lady who was on suicide supervision due to suicidal ideations. She was on my caseload when I worked in the girls unit; I had developed a rapport with her.

I entered the counseling room that was adjacent to the girls unit. Maria was sitting with hands crossed, refusing to speak to anyone and her eyes consumed with sadness and depression. I slowly walked into the office and saw Maria facing the wall opposite the door, attempting to avoid any eye contact with me or anyone else. I quietly sat on a chair across from her.

I asked in a concerned manner, "Hey, Maria what's going on?" She responded by keeping her hands crossed. She turned her head, but kept the rest of her body turned away from me and the door.

As she turned away she said, "I ain't talking to you, or anybody else. I just want to be left alone."

I made several other attempts to get her to talk to me, but she just ignored me. After ten minutes of attempting to get her to speak, I decided to go outside the parameters of crisis counseling. "Maria, I am leaving, and I will leave you alone, but I just have one important question to ask you."

She took a deep breath and said, "What is it?"

"Well, I was wondering... I was wondering if you passed gas."

"What?" She responded with a perplexed expression.

"Yeah, I am asking you if you farted!" Without changing the expression on my face, "Because I know it wasn't me." I paused and then even more seriously asked her, "Was it you?"

She turned her head and relaxed her crossed arms. She began showing signs of restrained laughter.

"So, was it you? You can tell me!"

She turned toward me and broke out with uncontrollable laughter, saying, "You are crazy, Mr. Ruan!"

From that point on, I was able to speak with her. The outrageous remark broke through her wall. She had no idea what to do with my approach. All I needed was for her to laugh, and that got her to talk about her reasons for feeling suicidal. I do not know why I said that at the time, but it worked. I knew I needed to make a move to get her off balance in order to get her to talk. It is the same thing in martial arts: the opponent needs to be off balance, or open, in order to execute a certain technique.

Another form of healthy humor I witnessed was in my travels to Native American reservations. I have always enjoyed Indian humor, a form of humor that is not abrasive, but more focused on the human experience. The humor is shared in a community context and inclusive of all ages. In Navajo Land, some of the most evolved holy people that are healers are like stand-up comedians. They have the ability to make people laugh, to teach people through humor, and help them relax. During an intense ceremony, humor puts people back on track.

A sense of humor is the ability to laugh at yourself and to laugh at situations we cannot control. A healthy sense of humor is not power-driven or focused on a person's shortcomings. When we laugh at ourselves, we create a healthy release of unnecessary tension. A sense of humor makes life lighter and reminds us not to take ourselves so seriously.

Sensory Acuity

I remember reading about the founder of Aikido, Morihei Ueshiba, who had the ability to see what his attacker was going to do in the form of white light, before the attacker executed a move. He was able to counter the move before anything occurred. Sensory acuity is the ability to sense when something is about to happen, to sense the unseen paying close attention to our gut feeling. Sensory acuity will never fail us if we listen to it. In general, people who work in the trenches, probation, law enforcement, social work, and youth workers, all have a well-developed sensory acuity.

Several street youth I have come across have often shared stories of how their intuition warned of potential danger. When they ignored their intuition, they paid the consequences. I have heard the same scenario from parents, police officers, probation officers, and social workers. Their instincts are what assisted in their survival. Intuition is interrelated to people's language, body cues, and facial expressions.

Learn to listen to what you sense when you meet someone for the first time. I feel it is something that anyone can develop. We just need to be patient and practice.

Body Language

Another part of sensory acuity is what we project. When I work in juvenile hall or conduct a group in state prison, my body language must communicate confidence and a calm state. If I carry myself with fear and insecurity, I will not be effective; it opens the door to manipulation and unnecessary conflict. The same idea applies on the street: if a person walks in fear, they will attract the attention of predator behavior.

It is important how we project our body language, facial expressions, and tone of voice. Sometimes individuals will express fear, doubt, and disgust to their clients or a group of people. They try to pretend that they are sincere, but the nonverbal language and their energy scream their truth. That energy can be read and processed in a matter of minutes. It is important how we communicate because our clients are studying us. Some of our clients have learned to quickly read an individual for survival. In nature and with people, fear can be felt, instantly.

Unpredictable Counseling

Every individual is different. One approach might work for one person, but it might make another person rebel and shut down even more from your well-intended efforts. A client might need you to be firm and brutally honest with them. They might be upset and their ego slightly bruised, but they will work with it and make an effort to create some adjustments in their life. Every now and then, this can be the best approach.

Be aware, that a client of yours has a spirit that might be so damaged, that open honesty might just push them away because it is too much for them to handle. Give them just enough. If it is too much, you could lose them. Think about what is going to help in the long run, not what is going to make you feel better in the moment? It is a judgment call.

Negative Statements and Counter Statements

I had many kids tell me how they were having a great time being in a gang and getting high. "Nobody could get me out of a gang, not my parents, not the schools, and not you, mister." How do we handle such conviction?

I have come across many of these cases. My strategy is not to fight them and make them see things my way, but to help them realize the ramifications of their behavior. If they choose a way of life that is destructive, there are only two things I can continually do: talk to them and pray.

Change will occur in an individual's life, if they want it to happen. They must be passionate and fierce about wanting it; not everyone is at that level. There are a lot of factors that must be considered in order for people to allow change to occur in their lives. It's not that simple. For some people, the change takes longer than others. That is the reality. We can speed up the process by motivating our clients and selling them on their potential; transformation takes work. From that point on, it all depends on the individual's determination and motivation.

Sometimes you get an individual who is stubborn and thinks they know everything. For these kinds of clients I review what I am going to say to them beforehand. In my mind, I rehearse how I will counter their negative remarks and their attitudes. This way I will be prepared to deal with every possible negative remark. I ask the individual specific questions and learn to counter their negative remarks and pinpoint their generalizations. It is helpful to use words to redirect them during these conversations, such as: *regardless, nevertheless, yet,* and *however.* These words are like Aikido wrist-locks that change the direction of the verbal energy.

Once redirected, the following pieces of the conversation often reveal your client's heart and mind: the use of rude, harsh statements by the client are intended to shock and push the counselor or mentor away from dealing with the heart of the matter. Often, when this is done the counselor's patience is tested and their objective is successful. Some clients are skillful in using such negative statements for their benefit. Those who face these remarks need to learn to use the energy of the youth to redirect them. The counselor or mentor needs to tap into the core of what is really occurring and try not to get lost in the superficial behavior the troubled youth is displaying.

Below are some examples of statements I have come across in my work. Study and use them to your advantage. I also share some examples of counter statements redirecting negative remarks:

❖ Youth Statement: "Mr. Ruan, I do not care what you say or do. I plan on being in a gang for life. I will probably go to prison, and I will probably be a gang member until somebody takes me out."

  ▪ Counter Statement: *That's okay, if you want to die before you reach 18. That's okay if you never want to be with a woman for the rest of your life, and if you want to live in a cell the size of your bathroom with somebody else. Are you ready for that? I am not saying you can't handle it, you can adjust. But why live a life like that?*

❖ Youth Statement: "Hey Man! Whatever happens, happens!"

  ▪ Counter statement: *Yes, whatever happens will happen! But why does it have to happen to everyone in your family and to the people who love you while it's happening to you?"*

❖ Youth Statement: "We all have to die some time!"

  ▪ Counter statement: *Sure, but why die so soon? And why do you make your family experience a slow death of everything you put them through?*

❖ Youth statement: "You can't trust anybody because they will backstab you!"

  ▪ Counter Statement: *Nobody? Can you be more specific? Has there ever been a time when you trusted somebody and they came through for you in a healthy manner? Is there a person who has never stabbed you in the back? Is that possible? What did that person do or say to gain that trust? Is it possible that there are people you could trust and who can help you?*

❖ Youth Statement: "I am going to be in a gang for life!"

  ▪ Counter statement: *Okay if that is what you want. But why does your family have to pay for your mistakes and be in pain for life? Don't you love your family? Why do you hurt them? What has to happen in order for you to stop hurting yourself and others?*

❖ Youth statement: "What do you know? You have never been through what I must go through every day."

  ▪ Counter Statement: *Regardless of whether I have not gone through your experiences, I am not blind to your pain. It doesn't take a genius to see what you are doing to yourself and your future. You just keep pushing people away. Why do you do that? Don't you know that people love you and want you to be happy? This is about you, not me.*

- ❖ Youth Statement: "I make more money selling drugs in one day than you make in a month."
    - ▪ Counter statement: *Yes, you make lots of money, but are you at peace? Does your work make you happy? What price do you pay for being a drug dealer? What price does the community pay? How many people do you think you have strung out on drugs? How many families have you ruined? Does that matter to you? What if somebody in your family became addicted? How would you feel about that?"*

Connecting

A connection with your client is vital. Once a relationship is in place, healing and learning is able to excel. Below are examples of what can be done to develop leverage.

- ❖ Parents
    - ➤ Develop a relationship with the parents/guardian of the youth you are working with. This helps to understand and assess the child's needs. Most parents will be helpful and pleased that you are trying to help their child.
    - ➤ You also need parental support. It makes it very difficult to be manipulated by your client if you have a solid relationship with their family. Comprehensive support is necessary in the healing process.

❖ Developing Juice
> If it is appropriate, visit them in Juvenile Hall, the hospital and at home. Be there when they need you. This is what I call "developing juice." Send them encouragement during difficult times. This creates a sense of loyalty. Most youth will never forget your loyalty.
> I have witnessed field probation officers go into hard-core neighborhoods, and literally, diffuse potentially volatile incidents by using the leverage they had developed. There are times when you might need to cash in this leverage during dangerous situations.
> On a personal note, I was able to stop riots in institutions because of the "juice" I developed with the youths. On several occasions they warned me of possible dangerous situations that could have easily surfaced.

❖ Confidentiality
> It is important that whatever the youth communicates to you, that you keep it confidential. Tell them upfront if there is information given that you might have to report to your supervisors, such as; child molestation, abuse or criminal confessions.
> As a counselor, I was required by law to report criminal offenses and child abuse. I always informed the youth during each session in case I had to report something they told me.
> Youth will gravitate towards authentic communication and selfless actions.

❖ Personal Problems
  ➢ Avoid taking out your personal problems on your clients. Leave personal problems at home or outside-of-your-environment. I have observed numerous people take out their problems on the very youth they are trying to help. Often, they are not aware of it. Always deal with your problems on your own time. It is unfair to your clients. Be there for them.

CHAPTER 13 FOCUS

The principles and philosophy of martial arts can be useful when working with people in diverse environments. This philosophy is an approach of respect. It encompasses accountability, dignity, and reflection in redirecting youth violence. To be effective, one must be flexible, possess a balanced approach, a protective understanding, sensory acuity, sense of humor, knowing how to redirect negative comments. All of these elements will assist in connecting with your clients and leading them into transformational behavior. This form of redirection has to do with not allowing your ego to dictate your response, but utilizing clever techniques that will provide beneficial results.

CHAPTER XIV

FREEDOM FROM
THE COMFORT ZONE

TO SUCCESSFULLY COMPLETE THE *Journey to the Mountain Within,* it is essential to continuously aspire to improve and enhance the way we live. Our situation in life is a reflection of our thoughts, beliefs, and upbringing. If not guided properly, these influences can impede our innate development. This is why it is easy to accept mediocrity and to endure a way of life *below* our potential. Our inner voice reminds us of the pitfalls, accepting a perspective of fear and complacency. To overcome these road blocks, we need a fearless, resilient attitude of possibility. This attitude needs to be nurtured and maintained. That is why setting goals outside the Comfort Zone produces a journey of knowledge, confidence, and happiness. The following is an example of moving beyond the disempowering Comfort Zone.

As a high school track and field runner, I recall reading a magazine article about the breaking of the four-minute-mile record. Prior to 1954, the thought of doing this seemed impossible. Many attempts were made, but no human had yet to run the mile in record

249

breaking time. This mindset was shattered when Roger Bannister from Great Britain, a medical student at the time, ran the mile in less than four minutes: 3 minutes, 59.4 seconds.

When he broke the four-minute-mile barrier, the world was in awe. "I had no doubt, the idea of *not* running in less than four minutes was ridiculous…a mental block established to explain failure." Bannister simply refused to accept that breaking the four-minute-mile record was impossible.

Often, we get trapped in mental blocks, a limited mindset that becomes normalized if not challenged. This Comfort Zone is a form of acceptance of mediocrity that holds us back in life. Bannister is a prime example of success when breaking through a self-imposed obstacle.

This state of mind is sustained by levels of fear and sometimes, trauma. When an individual is stuck in the Comfort Zone, a paralysis of fear becomes rooted. The fear does not allow the individual to develop and grow, having a paralyzing effect on a person's ability to move forward. Fear has many faces: fear of the unknown, fear of success, fear of change, fear of failure, and the list goes on. Many situations can be defined as Comfort Zones: domestic violence, drugs, alcohol abuse, negative relationships, dead-end jobs, and incarceration, to name a few.

Another example of someone breaking out of their stagnation is Tony Hernandez; I mentored Tony when he was incarcerated at Donavan State Prison, in San Diego, California. This person was not a famous example of breaking through like Bannister, but instead, an ordinary example of the process one must go through to go beyond an unpleasant reality.

When I met him he was thirty years old, serving time for his drug use and gang involvement. Tony had been in and out of institutions since he was eleven. At a very young age, he began abusing drugs and alcohol, and then became a heroin addict as a young adult. Along the way, he became a member of his neighborhood street gang and experienced the progression from juvenile institutions to State Prison.

Most of his childhood and young adulthood were spent in institutions. One of the major factors leading to his problems was an absent biological father he never met, and a single mother who was gone most of the time, working odd jobs with low pay and long hours. His neighborhood was socially and economically deprived with drugs, alcohol, and gang activity dominating the community. It appeared as if his upbringing groomed him for failure. Like most people who grow up within all of these elements, Tony had a difficult time overcoming unrelenting negative forces.

I met Tony through my friend Mary, a correctional counselor at Donavan State Prison in Southern California. We had worked together when I was in the Orange County Probation Department. She was assigned to train me when I first started. We later became close friends and Mary asked if I would mentor Tony. "Louie this guy has it, I think you could really help him, and he could help the kids that you work with." Mary was aware that I mentored numerous teens, yet I had never mentored an adult gang member before. After much thought, I agreed.

I began writing Tony letters of encouragement. I wanted to see where he was with his healing. We communicated through letters and with a few collect calls from prison. I sent him books I believed would assist in his healing. He was grateful for the books and the letters. Tony would respond to each book I sent him with a well thought-out analysis. He sent me a few of his favorite books, which I enjoyed as well. We had in common the love of books and knowledge and it was impressive that Tony was self-taught. I wanted to see where he was at with his healing process and if he was interested in shifting his lifestyle.

After three months of correspondence, I felt he was willing to do the work to change, but I needed to see if he was serious about moving forward. I decided to visit him at Donavan State Prison. Located a few miles away from the Mexican border, the prison was situated in a rural part of southeast San Diego County. It took me two hours to drive to this isolated location.

When I arrived at the prison, I checked in at the front office. I waited until a correctional officer searched me and placed several of my personal items in plastic bags. After that, I waited again until it was time for me to be escorted to the visiting room. I found myself becoming impatient with the constant sitting.

With boredom and impatience as motivators, I started to look around at the people visiting other inmates. They were mostly people of color, waiting to visit their loved ones. I saw mothers, grandmothers, grandfathers, girlfriends, wives, friends, and other family members. It reminded me of how love can be unconditional. I started to wonder how many of the people around me went through this long process of visiting an inmate, regularly.

After experiencing body searches, enduring long waits, and hearing large electrical gates opening and closing, I finally reached his visiting room. I was immediately aware of the constant supervision from vigilante correctional officers. Every move and gesture made was watched from the gun towers, cameras, or correctional officers. This was intimidating.

As I waited in the prison waiting room, I wondered what Tony would look like, never having met him. Our communication was solely through letters and occasional collect phone calls. I recall a time when he had made several attempts to call me and I had been out of town working. A few weeks had passed of missed phone calls when I did finally make contact with him. "Hey man! You really don't have to do this," he said in a medium pitched, raspy voice, distinctive for a guy doing prison time.

"Do what?" I asked.

"You don't have to talk to me if you don't want to ... I know you're really busy, and I am just an inmate."

"Hey, hey... take it easy. Yes, I am busy, but I want to do this. You need to be a little patient with people." I tried to tell him this as lightly as possible. He responded with laughter that broke the tension.

What impressed me the most about Tony was his well-developed intellect. While in prison he read many books of substance on history, politics, current events, and spirituality. His favorite television shows were always on Public Broadcasting or the History Channel. In our conversations, he had interesting things to say about all subjects. At times I thought I was talking to an articulate college graduate.

While in the visiting room, I thought about all those things. It was a stale and cold environment with mostly physically fit young and a few older men who possessed that hard-prison look with tattoos covering the upper body and neck. The inmates sat with their families while being closely supervised by vigilant correctional officers strapped with intimidating handguns and fully equipped accessory belts that held pepper spray, a baton, handcuffs, and a radio; ready for battle.

As I took my mind away from the visiting room dynamics and waited patiently for Tony's arrival, I imagined him being of medium height with long hair. I pictured him as someone who was ready to get out of prison but I was wrong. Out of one of the doors walked out a Chicano inmate who was athletically lean, tall and prison gangster bald. His blue, state-provided creased long-sleeved shirt concealed his tattooed body. Tony was thirty, but looked as if he were in his early twenties.

He walked to my area and said with a slight smile, "Are you Louie?"

I nodded and stood up to shake his hand. I noticed he had big hands like a boxer that helped him to protect himself on the streets and in prison. As we began our visit, it was easy to talk. He seemed like a relative, someone I knew before. I bought him a pizza, available for the visitors and inmates. We continued to talk while we ate.

During the middle of the visit, I told Tony that I was willing to work with him for a year. I shared with him that I had put much thought and prayer into the idea of being a mentor, and that everyone needs one.

Mentors are needed to help, support and assist in the development of an individual. In a healthy environment, a person will experience numerous positive and empowering mentors. Through my life I had several mentors that added to my life experience and knowledge. For gang members and for Latino males who are stuck in the system like Tony, most of the mentors they have only reinforce and perpetuate a life of violence or crime. I felt it was my responsibility to do my best to be a positive and healthy example for Tony. That was my intent: understanding that the learning and development had to be mutual, not something I could do for him. After my semi-rehearsed speech, he smiled and thanked me.

After discussing the details of the mentorship, I asked him what plans he had upon his release. With a glow on his face he tells me, "I am going to stay clean from drugs, get a job, eat as much as I want, fix-up my car, sleep on a comfortable bed, and be with my girlfriend as much as possible... things are going to be great!"

As he talked, I could not help but get a strong gut feeling about the reality of his future. I believed he was capable of breaking his negative cycle, but I also knew it would not be easy. Many men who are involved in the prison system find themselves recidivating. I knew that Tony had stayed clean and out of trouble while he was in prison, but I still felt he was going to be seriously tested.

After he finished telling me his plans, I looked at him and calmly pointed out, "It can be rough out there, be careful... I will be there to help you though." He had a hopeful smile and continued to discuss more of his detailed plans beyond the prison walls.

A year later, after serving a three-year sentence, he was released and he asked me to pick him up. When I arrived at the prison gate, he was outside waiting patiently. I could tell he was nervous and anxious about being outside the prison walls.

He carefully stepped into my car and we drove north to his girlfriend's house in Orange County, California. Along the way, we drove by Camp Pendleton Marine Corp Base located amongst rolling hills and vast land adjacent to the picturesque California Coast separated by the 5 Freeway. As we drove down the freeway, a red-tailed hawk flew above us, a sign that Tony would have spiritual support at his disposal.

Breaking Through the Barrier of the Comfort Zone

Seven years later from the day I picked up Tony at Donavan Prison, he was visiting me in my living room during a humid evening in Pacoima, California. We sat eating *carne asada burritos* and drinking cold iced tea. I thought about how one year of mentoring transpired into seven years and how things had changed. I had moved after my divorce, and Tony was no longer with the girlfriend from his prison days. He had connected with another woman who was more understanding and a positive balance for him. His new girlfriend, Caroline came from a solid family; she had advanced degrees in teaching and art history. She was a grounded, educated, confident, and very supportive of Tony's healing. He finally had the stability he yearned for in a partner.

I looked at Tony and realized how much had happened in those seven years. I remembered vividly the time I picked him up from Donavan Prison and within that time period, he had experienced events that could have shattered the average person. During that time, he stayed away from Donovan State Prison only to return two times to Chino State Prison for parole violations. He relapsed five times, was kicked out of his old girlfriend's house four times, had dropped out of rehab twice, attempted suicide twice, faced a lot of inner emotional pain, and went through a deep depression. He had hit the lowest of the low during the first half of those seven years. Tony's trauma was deep and his healing was going to take time.

I remembered that first visit with him in the prison visiting room, his words, and the eager look on his face when he told me he was going to cease abusing drugs and stay away from prison. I knew he was going to face numerous obstacles, but I also knew that sharing my insights would only have killed his hopeful spirit. That was not what he needed. He needed someone to believe in him and give encouragement, regardless of what he was about to go through.

One thing I learned is that sometimes people have to figure things out for themselves. If I would have told him what I really thought about what he would go through, he would have only seen me as a negative and non-supportive person. He needed someone whom he could trust and who believed in him.

Tony was able to learn several hard lessons. For the last three of those seven years, he was able to become sober from heroin and free from gang violence. He managed to stay away from prison and his relapses were further and further apart. To me, he became a success! Tony's Comfort Zone was one of the most challenging I have witnessed. Based on his background, he was destined to become another statistic, just another Chicano drug addict/gang member, kept in an over-crowded prison system. Fortunately, he was able to create his own destiny.

In my work, I have seen examples of people who have been successful in staying out of their Comfort Zone. Once they set their mind, they were able to accomplish something that was unique for them. We all have challenges to overcome. Yet we possess all the necessary tools within, to overcome any obstacle that presents itself.

Levels of the Comfort Zone

Level 1: Grounded Expectations

It is important to have a realistic view of what life is like outside of the Comfort Zone. For example, I met this man named Paul at a men's retreat who was in an unhealthy marriage. His wife was having multiple affairs with other men and abusing drugs. He'd had enough and decided to get a divorce. Paul believed that once he was divorced, things were going to be great: date women, travel, and be happy again.

Eventually he was able to do all those things. It took him over three years until he was ready to date again and to be in healthy place for his aspirations beyond the divorce. First, he needed time to heal. He attended Native American healing ceremonies and men's support groups. Such changes cannot happen immediately, but with time his pain began to dissipate.

High levels of anticipation of expected outcomes will lead to emotional disappointment if not guided by real and grounded expectations. When Tony was in prison, he believed everything was going to be identical to his expectations. In time, he realized that life outside of prison is difficult and his expectations were not identical to reality. Life has its own current.

Level 2: The Honeymoon phase

This is the time when people get a taste of being outside the Comfort Zone. They are in the early stages of it and things are still fresh and new. The true colors of this level have not revealed itself yet, but they will in time. The honeymoon of the Comfort Zone is usually a short-lived.

At twenty years old I moved out of my parent's home in San Diego and moved to Los Angeles. At first, I was elated and during the first few months, overjoyed to finally be on my own. But after a while, I missed my family and realized I was responsible for situations I had not considered when I was living with my parents. It became difficult to be on my own. I spent many lonely evenings longing for my mom's warm meals and to be around my family. I had to cook for myself, and when my financial aid was delayed, I had to *tough it out* by eating beans and water. Other times, I just went hungry. I had to be patient until I was able to get enough money to provide for my own basic needs. My parents were unable to bail me out and I did not want to worry them. My expectations were not aligned to the reality I was facing.

When Tony was released, everything appeared to be great. He was happy to be in a non-prison environment, to be with his girlfriend, to play with his daughter, and to do what he pleased.

259

Tony no longer had a prison correctional officer constantly watching him and telling him what to do. He was on his way to creating the life he had always wanted.

Level 3: Reality

The honeymoon has terminated and it is time to experience the reality of being out of the restrictions of the old way of living. This is where we must get the strength and the openness to become familiar with the flip-side of being out, like getting used to living in a foreign country where everything is new and unfamiliar. The stress level is elevated because of the need for constant adjustment. Some people move through it gracefully, while others have a hard time with change. What will manifest during this phase is the difficulty dealing with being outside of what is familiar.

In Tony's case, after almost a month, reality began to set in and his world began to change. His girlfriend was getting frustrated; he was not communicating. She felt Tony was not being sensitive to her needs and the needs of the family. A large portion of their relationship was spent in verbal conflict, arguing about common male/female issues.

At times, Tony took her behavior and words the wrong way; he was not used to dealing with that type of conflict, and lacked reference points. He had no problem dealing with potentially violent inmates or communicating seasoned gang members, but his relationship with his girlfriend was difficult. At the same time, his girlfriend was not used to interacting with a man living in the same space with her. Tony had always been away and in prison and they needed to learn how to live together.

An additional pressure was to find a job. With a prison record, potential employers were suspicious. Another factor adding to his stress was the difficulty in dealing with a non-prison structured environment. He was not accustomed to dealing with stress and rejection outside of the gang and institutional environment. All this stress that most people deal with day-to-day was tenfold for Tony. The mind begins to question and doubt the importance of leaving what was safe, routine, and familiar.

Level 4: Return to Comfort Zone

At this point, the individual might begin thinking: *I guess it wasn't that bad back then.* Doubts set in and begin to test the decisions that have been made to leave the Comfort Zone in the first place. What is needed here is more patience by identifying the needs that were met.

Returning to the Comfort Zone may happen, and it may happen more than once, becoming a revolving door. Sometimes people need to experience certain scenarios over and over again to understand them well. But this situation might provide an opportunity to evaluate the reasons they returned. This is a time of introspection and self-evaluation, where returnees need to decide if this is how they want to live their life, or whether it is fulfilling a need they have not yet identified.

The path appears to be easy on the surface, but that image is misleading. This path goes back into stagnation where growth ceases to exist. There, the only growth that occurs is as a witness, not as an active participant.

When someone is only a witness to life, the experience is incomplete. It is like watching someone else go to the Polynesian Islands through a television reality show, trying to experience what they are experiencing through the big screen. Instead of living life to the fullest and experiencing a way of life they love, they experience it through observation, relinquishing their own experiences and chance for happiness.

When someone truly is a participant in life, lessons are experienced at all levels. The mind, body and spirit need it for lessons to be instilled and rooted. Learning occurs in all modalities: auditory, visual, and kinesthetic. In order for the individual to stay outside of the Comfort Zone, they must take steps as a complete engaged participant. As an active participant, we learn in a profound manner, and faster. Only then, do we have a complete experience instead of one-dimensional. Staying in the phase of the Comfort Zone, the individual begins to destroy what they have built during this brief period of freedom.

In the peak of his drama, I received a collect call from Tony while in County Jail. He explained how he was relieved to be back. He said that it was too difficult out in the world; in prison, at least he knew what to expect and how to survive. I knew that at that point, his mind had begun to yearn for the emotional familiarity and safety he had been conditioned for. Thoughts like: *Hey, prison was not all that bad. At least I was someone in there. At least I knew what to expect, and could deal with in that world.*

The unfamiliarity of society produced a different form of stress in him. I've known many young men who were so institutionalized that being out in the free world was overwhelming and difficult for them to overcome. Young men and women are often released from prison with little or no resources and are expected to prevail on their own. That is why some may become repeat offenders, just so they can return to the system.

Level 5: The Crossroads

This phase is the breaking point; it breaks the barriers of the Comfort Zone. This phase is the most difficult because it is the turning point where spiritual, emotional, and mental growth proliferates. If the individual chooses to move towards another stage in their life, it is important to accept the challenges and to be aware of the level of work that is required. At this point, a decision must be made.

Often people are not ready to make a commitment to leave their misery. They either move toward leaving their unpleasant situation, or stay in it until they are forced out. It is up to the individual and everyone has their own pace in dealing with positive change. Even though we do not like being in a place where our potential is inactive, people will spend a lifetime putting up with it because it is safe and familiar.

I recall this happening to me when I started the *Beyond Limits Program*. Friends and co-workers were telling me, "You are crazy... taking gang members and murderers to the mountains!" Another comment was, "Louie, you have never run a non-profit organization... you don't know the first thing about this!" Another negative comment a friend shared with me once was, "How are you going to get the money to finance the trips?" After hearing these negative remarks, I began to doubt myself. I began thinking, that maybe they are right, perhaps I am just dreaming and being unrealistic.

Fortunately, a confidence within me overpowered those negative comments and gave me the motivation to manifest my dream. If I would have listened to everyone and their doubts, I would never have learned the valuable tools of building an outdoor youth program. I would have remained in the safety of my Comfort Zone, would have missed the opportunity to grow, and would have denied myself some of the greatest memories of my life.

Level 6: Making a Decision

Perhaps the individual enjoys the Comfort Zone and does not want to do anything about it. If it is limiting and not in their best interest, they must decide if moving beyond the misery is what they want. It is decision time. Reaching a conclusion or making up one's mind must happen at this point.

To move forward, they need to accept the fact that leaving the Comfort Zone is going to be difficult, and uncomfortable. When people have the perception that it is going to be an easy transition, they are setting themselves up for disappointment. If the acceptance of difficulty is present, the individual can prepare and begin taking the necessary steps toward transition.

When I spoke with Tony while in prison during our initial visit, he had a romantic point of view of what was to come. If he knew the hardship he would go through maybe things would have been different for him. It is hard to say. He did not know what he was about to go through; all he understood was that he wanted to change his life. Tony struggled, but in the end, prevailed.

When anyone goes through a traumatic event, it takes time for the person to heal completely. Sometimes a person's healing is never complete. If that happens, what is important is that progress was made. Progression is movement in the right direction.

We all have our challenges and situations that impede our growth. Some of them are very obvious, while others are subtle. It is up to us to assist the people we work with and ourselves to go beyond a life that is beyond fear and stagnation. It means different things to different people and it is important to identify our own personal issues.

In my experience, it is the Great Spirit that will often place situations in front of me to test my inability to move towards a better life. If I refuse to go beyond it, the situation will become fierce. It has always been up to me to choose what to do; everyone has a choice. Completing this process will bring forth many gifts of self-knowledge and awareness.

Inherently, people do not want to change because it is too difficult. It is easier to be complacent, disregarding the damage it is causing in a person's life. Change takes commitment, not only in words, but in congruent actions with the mind, body and soul. The phenomena of the Comfort Zone can be enticing and deceiving. It projects the illusion of fate, but we must know better. It is not our fate to be miserable. We are all worthy of having a healthy and prosperous life.

CHAPTER 14 FOCUS

Another level of reaching the *Journey to the Mountain Within* is to move past the Comfort Zone. This mindset is a place of mediocrity where growth and development ceases to flourish. People can easily remain in a place of misery because it is comfortable and habit forming. Some individuals will never leave it because of fear of the unknown. Going beyond this stagnation is not an easy task, but a process which produces confidence, wisdom, and happiness. One way to move past the stagnation is to develop a committed and focused point of view with the support and guidance of knowledgeable mentors. Experiences become lessons learned and a source of inspiration. *Live and explore your innate potential.*

EPILOGUE

I WANT TO THANK YOU, for choosing to read *Journey to the Mountain Within.* The stories and experiences in this book have come from my interaction with young people and their families in some of the poorest, marginalized, and ignored communities in Southern California and within Native America Nations. This chosen path has been one of many challenges. That is why I felt it was important to highlight the complicated but insightful stories I have come across regarding of what young people and families must endure to survive. These relationships taught me the most; they were rich with lessons about the human mind and behavior. The difficult experiences made my heart heavy and compelled me to question the purpose of my chosen profession. Yet, this interaction made my commitment stronger and armed me with unique experiences and wisdom to assist future clients.

This journey brought forward the understanding that God gave us the special gift of intelligence and free-will. If used correctly, our mind has the capability to find solutions for any human obstacle.

We have the intelligence to improve any situation, for others, or in our own personal lives. Sometimes it is as simple of asking the correct specific questions that leads to an advantageous outcome. At the same time, this intelligence can be manifested in a creative program, a unique way in approaching your clients, and the necessary steps to find happiness.

We also have the free-will to make our own decisions. To lead our lives any direction we choose. To take risks that will be used as a learning tool or to unfold our personal version of success. Each decision has a conclusion that is seen and unseen. We have the power and creativity to create unique, effective, long term programs to assist our young people. It's time!

It was my free-will and intelligence that took me through this path. I am grateful for every moment of this path. Through this process, I was able to connect with people from my past that were present during pivotal times in my life. I reconnected with old mentors, family members, various mentees, and past friendships. These particular individuals I write about were very insightful and made a huge impact on my character and my beliefs on what works and what doesn't work with youth.

For the young people that I mentored, I wanted to show a different side of them that most people cannot or refused to see. Often, when people see a young man with tattoos and a bald head, they may feel fear or see danger. Rarely do they see the uniqueness, intelligence or compassion that they might posses. I wrote this book to open their eyes. It was my intent to honor all the people I have worked with throughout my life.

◎ ◎ ◎

Martial Arts Mentors

With the support of my two sons, I joined a martial arts school in 2007. The style we study is called Kuk Sool Kwan and it is a Korean Martial Art that originates from the Korean Royal Court. It is a comprehensive martial art that includes Hapkido wristlocks, break-falls, ground fighting, Judo, kickboxing, weapons training, aerial kicks and Kung Fu movements.

In 2011, for two years, I trained in kickboxing with Coach Thourn Heng also know as Coach 2Win, at South Coast Martial Arts in Costa Mesa, California. One of the reasons I returned to martial arts was to spend more quality time with my sons. As a divorced father, I needed something that would reinforce the bond I have with them. My boys love to see me spar and get great joy seeing me fall flat on my face when I am trying a dynamic kick with my overweight body. Thanks to my sons, my love for martial arts has been rekindled after many years of not training.

During the research of *Journey to the Mountain Within*, I decided to contact Terry Crook. I realized what he did for me and other youth was a noble act, and I had a compelling need to thank him. After utilizing the internet and seeking the help of a childhood friend and martial artist Brason Lee, I was able to locate Terry. I was a bit nervous before calling him. I was afraid he would not remember me or maybe he was not interested in hearing from me again. My worries were plentiful. Finally I just called him. He answered the phone and I said, "Terry, this is Luis Ruan, one of your original students from the Cuahtli Dojo in National City. Do you remember me?"

"Of course I remember you! How are you? Does your brother Carlos still have asthma; I remember your father put him in karate to help him."

I was impressed he remembered us so well. "No Terry, he no longer has asthma. He is a lawyer and is doing well with his family."

After catching up on our current lives and discussing the lives of the other students who had trained with us, I communicated the following:

> Terry, I want to thank you for your dedication with me and the other guys you trained in karate at the old dojo. I want you to know because of the support and dedication you provided, I was able to mentor hundreds of youth the last twenty-five years and I am writing a book about it.
>
> Many of the kids I grew up with in my neighborhood did not do as well. Some of them have ended up dead or in prison. I just want you to know that your efforts had a major influence in my life and the life of others... thank you Terry.

He was quiet for a few seconds and said, "That's why I drove you guys to martial arts twice a week because I was afraid of what might happen to you and your brother if I didn't." I heard a silent pause on the phone. I choked up with emotion. I never knew he felt that way.

Because of these great deeds of my mentors, I want to honor my martial art instructors; Terry Crook, John Murphy, (Wada Kai

Japanese style), and Orned "Chicken" Gabriel from the United Karate Federation, who allowed me to train in his studio for a year without asking for a penny. Also, Mr. Wong (Aikido), Sensei Rod Kobashi (Aikido), and my current teachers Master Mike Dunchuk from Kuk Sool Kwan and Thourn Heng, kickboxing and boxing coach. Mr. Wong and Sensei Kobashi have since passed on, yet their work has left a profound impression on me and on others. Thank You!

Due to the influences of my early martial arts mentors, I have mentored hundreds of young people. These mentors taught me that redirecting energy may be applied to many life situations and that the martial arts philosophy is a metaphor for experiencing a full and healthy life.

Probation

I am grateful for the ten years in the Orange County Probation Department. I learned many valuable lessons about the Juvenile Justice System, and the reasons young people get stuck in the revolving doors of incarceration. I feel it was perfect timing in my life to work in juvenile institutions; this experience prepared me for my work with youth outside of probation. I also went through numerous growing pains in the probation department that assisted in my career development.

However, I do not think too much has changed since I worked in probation. We still have a high incarceration rate. Latinos and African Americans are still the majority in prisons and juvenile institutions across the United States. Poor people still dominate the institutions as well. The belief that incarceration is the magic cure for youth violence is still dominant. And unfortunately, we have fewer programs available that deal with the core issues of why youth are sent to juvenile institutions in the first place.

As countless young men and women graduate to prison or die, incarceration has become an accepted way of life for some youth. For these reasons, I chose to take the path of trying to heal our young people. I learned that we first must understand the problem in order to create healing solutions. During my time in the probation department I was able to get a clear view of the problems, and had to leave to work on developing sustainable solutions.

Because of the many years doing this work, I often come across muscular tattooed young men who approach me in public and ask if I remember them when they were incarcerated in Orange County Probation facilities. It usually takes me awhile to make the connection because they look different from when they were teenagers and I have worked with such a vast number of youth within the system that my memory fails me.

One time, I was at Valley High School in Santa Ana, I had just completed an early evening running workout with several youth who were preparing to backpack Mt. Whitney. After the demanding workout I made my way to the parking lot. From the corner of my left eye I saw a muscular, rugged looking Latino man walk towards me with an intense look on his face. I found myself planning on how I was going to diffuse a possible confrontational situation. He stood in front of me and said, "Hey man! Did you work in probation?" I responded with a serious tone, "Yes, I worked there for ten years."

He then relaxed his body language and took a deep breath and said, "Man, you were my counselor in Juvenile Hall. Don't you remember me? I tried to escape but I got caught and was sent to the California Youth Authority. You were always cool with me." The guy then shook my hand and eagerly walked with me to my car.

Situations like this were common when I lived in Santa Ana. It would happen at parks, at schools and sometimes even in grocery stores.

Beyond Limits

The *Beyond Limits* staff was a remarkable group of dedicated volunteers who assisted numerous youth taking part in exciting programs. They did this without accepting money from corporations that had ties to tobacco and alcohol companies. Today, when people tell me that the youth are out of control and there is nothing we can do to redirect their behavior, I just don't buy it. I have seen what is possible with my own eyes when people work together for a common goal. Prisons are full of young men and women who could have led positive and fulfilling lives, if only they had a fair opportunity to succeed.

Today, I am no longer active with the *Beyond Limits Program*; I dedicated eight years of my life to the program until I became very busy with workshops and consultant work. Fortunately, my good friend Mario Fuentes has taken the main leadership along with the assistance of Mary Lara and Carla Romo. They have been able to organize excursions for the youth in Orange and Los Angeles Counties. The program has hiked to Mt. Whitney many times, visited the Grand Canyon, had cultural exchanges on the Navajo Reservation, and backpacked in areas such as Northern California, Ute Reservation in Colorado and other locations.

Many of the youth who participated in our first trip are now serving as board members and staff on excursions. For example, Pedro Lopez from the second excursion became an active member of the program and has assisted in leading several backpacking excursions. During his senior year in high school, he was ranked Number 2 in Orange County for his cross-country distance running. Currently, he is on the *Beyond Limits* Board of Directors and a graduate from UC Davis. Several other participants have also graduated from college and are now serving throughout the community.

The program has been in existence for twenty years since the summer of 1991 when Octavio Gonzalez, Miguel Bernal, and I organized the first backpacking trip from Sequoia National Park to the summit of Mt. Whitney. Because of these excursions, hundreds of youth and families were impacted. Mario, Carla, and Mary have done an excellent job running the program. They have worked diligently to raise money to buy equipment and to pay for the logistics of expensive excursions.

Organizing these trips, recruiting youth, planning excursions, obtaining insurance, fund development, dealing with parents and schools is not an easy endeavor. I applaud their efforts and dedication. They have been successful in reaching numerous youth from inner cities and taking them to places they only dreamed about.

Indian Country

When gas was affordable, I would get in my van and drive twelve hours straight to attend a ceremony and visit close friends in Navajo Nation. However, because of the recent economy, I have not been able to travel and visit my friends in the Navajo Nation, South Dakota, Gila River or Canada for a number of years. I do miss certain things about these places, like the ability to hear actual silence, drives on highways with open scenery, breathing in fresh air, smelling the freshness of the earth, and walking where I could feel the natural power of the earth travel throughout my body. I miss going to ceremonies and leaving with a renewed perspective, being entertained by Native humor, and hearing the wisdom of the elders.

These encounters have been significant for me, and the lessons I learned in Indian Country has remained in my heart and mind. I enjoyed working in Indian Country; I met amazing people and had memorable experiences. Each Native Nation was unique. These experiences healed my heart, given me a greater understanding of my work, and I am blessed for having experienced such remarkable events.

Boyle Heights

From the moment I decided to set foot in Boyle Heights during the late nineties, I instinctively understood I would journey through a series of exceptional encounters with the folks there. Working in Boyle Heights was a homecoming for me. It was a comfortable breath of fresh air. The people had similar humor, language and cultural understanding.

I enjoyed it very much. Some of the original staff from IMPACTO Youth Leadership Program had taken other jobs or went on to continue with higher education. Alejandra Azucena is working as a social worker for the Los Angeles County Department of Social Services. Carlos Vasquez received his law degree and is on the Homeboy Industries Board of Directors. Dorwin Suarez graduated from California State Poly Pomona and just received her master's degree in social work. Raul *Rulies* Diaz works in the community and for Homeboy Industries. Christine Sanchez continues to work in the nonprofit world and spends as much time as possible with her two sons.

The IMPACTO youth in Boyle Heights left unforgettable memories in my heart. Today, some are parents and community leaders; many have graduated from universities. Several earned advanced degrees. They are the next generation of community leaders. When we reunite at graduations, weddings or community events we still possess that magical bond that was created many years ago in the old musty IMPACTO building on First Street in Boyle Heights.

The memories of all those wonderful young adults are certainly a high point in my life. I have never worked in a community where the youth and adults developed such a solid bond of trust and camaraderie. The experience in the Boyle Heights community was rich and profound – it was a perfect match for what my life needed at the time. We learned from each other, and we grew together.

Work Perspective

After my divorce in 2002, my youngest son Gabriel, who was 6-years-old at the time, innocently said to me, "Dad I am glad that you and mom got a divorce because now you spend more time with us... before, you were always working and gone."

His sincere observation really touched my heart. It is amazing how the divorce forced me to evaluate how I related to my sons and what type of father I wanted to be. I had been guilty of spending all of my time trying to save the world, but had neglected what was most important - my own family. One thing I learned from working with troubled kids is that consistent, healthy parenting produces emotionally balanced, secure kids who will not get involved in the juvenile justice system. I have been successful in being a father who is attentive, active and loving.

In summer 2009, I took my sons on a four-day backpacking trip in the Eastern Sierras. My sons did well during the trip. They often had to wait for me to catch up with their youthful pace while trekking up steep mountains. It reminded me of how my brother Carlos and I used to wait for my dad to catch up with us when we were teenagers during backpacking trips in the Cleveland National Forest in San Diego. Since my last trip with *Beyond Limits*, I had gained about 20 pounds and lacked the conditioning to hike up steep mountain trails with a full backpack. My sons did not care that I was slower than I used to be, they were just grateful to have a bonding experience with me.

That same year my oldest son Nico hiked the summit of Mt. Whitney with my friend Caroline Maxwell. They left the campsite at 5:30 a.m. and hiked twenty-two miles in fourteen hours. I stayed at the campsite with my younger son, Gabriel. We stayed busy by taking a four-mile hike and fishing with his homemade fishing pole. Despite feeling happy, my thoughts were locked on Nico hiking that mountain. I was proud, but as a father I wanted him to be safe and to have a positive experience as well. I must admit, I did my share of praying the entire day while he was hiking.

When he returned during the early evening, I noticed something different about my son. An internal shift had occurred by his involvement in the hike. I saw it in his energy, and the way he walked. I asked him, "Did you feel the power of the mountain?"

He looked at me and said with a warm smile, "Dad that was a really tough hike. When I was at the top I just wanted to come down."

I was so proud of him. He had hiked a mountain that his grandfather and his father had climbed. When I get in better physical condition we plan to backpack to the summit as a family. Over the years, I have learned the best thing I can do for the world is to be the best father I can be, and always put my family before my work.

Creator made my spiritual journey clear: the Great Spirit is my real boss. I believe my Creator talks through us when we are still, when our minds and hearts are pure and relaxed. The vessel of communication is expressed through our passion, dreams and thoughts; an internal compass of our life that maps out our purpose. We all have that compass, but we do not always use it.

I encourage you all to stop and listen …

CONTACT INFORMATION

For more information on the author's workshops and guest speaking, feel free to visit his website.

Website: luisruan.com